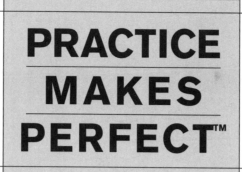

PRACTICE
MAKES
PERFECT™

Intermediate
Spanish Grammar

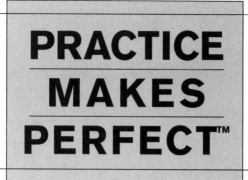

PRACTICE MAKES PERFECT™

Intermediate Spanish Grammar

Premium Second Edition

Gilda Nissenberg, PhD, Editor

Mc
Graw
Hill
Education

New York   Chicago   San Francisco   Athens   London   Madrid
Mexico City   Milan   New Delhi   Singapore   Sydney   Toronto

1 2 3 4 5 6 7 8 9   LHS   23 22 21 20 19 18

ISBN   978-1-260-12169-8
MHID   1-260-12169-0

e-ISBN 978-1-260-12170-4
e-MHID   1-260-12170-4

Interior design by Village Bookworks, Inc.

McGraw-Hill Education books are available at special quantity discounts to use as
premiums and sales promotions or for use in corporate training programs. To contact a
representative, please visit the Contact Us pages at www.mhprofessional.com.

McGraw-Hill Education Language Lab App

Audio recordings and flashcards are available to support your study of this book.
Go to the iTunes or Google Play app stores to download the free mobile app for
iOS and Android devices. A web version of this application is also available at
mhlanguagelab.com. See the inside front cover for more details about the features
of this app.

Contents

Preface

Practice Makes Perfect: Intermediate Spanish Grammar is designed to provide a user-friendly way to study and practice Spanish grammar at the intermediate level, especially for the self-taught learner. Users of this book will continue building their competency to communicate in Spanish.

Each chapter provides an easy way to understand explanations of grammar usage, by comparisons with English grammar when needed and clear examples that illustrate and clarify the grammatical explanations. The exercises that follow each section provide ample opportunity to practice with clear language and allow the self-learner to practice without having to search for many new words.

This new edition is supported by flash cards for all vocabulary lists throughout the book, as well as extensive streaming audio, available through the McGraw-Hill Education Language Lab app. The recordings provide answers to more than 120 exercises in this book. If your device has the capability, your own responses can be recorded to compare against the models provided by native-speakers.

The best way to acquire more knowledge and improve writing and speaking in Spanish is to practice and improve our own knowledge in order to communicate clearly with Spanish speakers.

Let's practice now!

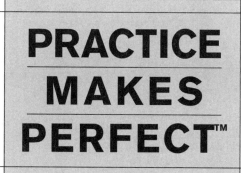

Intermediate
Spanish Grammar

Subject pronouns and the present tense

You have learned that in English and Spanish there are three grammatical persons—first, second, and third—in both singular and plural. Pronouns are used to replace the name of a person or object.

Subject pronouns

Let's review the subject pronouns in Spanish.

SINGULAR		PLURAL	
yo	*I*	**nosotros, -as**	*we*
tú	*you* (*fam.*)	**vosotros, -as**	*you* (*fam., masc., fem.*)
usted (Ud.)	*you* (*form.*)	**ustedes (Uds.)**	*you* (*form.*)
él	*he*	**ellos**	*they* (*masc.*)
ella	*she*	**ellas**	*they* (*fem.*)

The chart shows that, except the first person singular and the formal *you*, subject pronouns have both feminine and masculine forms. When a plural includes both masculine and feminine, the masculine form is used.

Marcos y Sandra son primos.	*Marcos and Sandra are cousins.*
Ellos son primos.	*They are cousins.*

The familiar plurals **vosotros** and **vosotras** are used in most regions of Spain; **ustedes** is the familiar plural used in most of the rest of the Spanish-speaking world. **Ud.** and **Uds.** are abbreviations of the formal subject pronouns. The context will clarify whether to use the familiar or the formal pronoun.

Señor López, ¿**usted** trabaja aquí?	*Mr. López, do you work here?*
Chicos, ¿**ustedes** salen ahora?	*Boys, are you leaving now?*

By addressing a man as **Señor**, you are showing this is a formal context. The word **chicos**, on the other hand, implies familiarity.

You probably have learned that subject pronouns are usually omitted in Spanish because the verb endings clarify both person and number. However, the subject pronoun is used if the subject is not clear, or if there is a need for emphasis.

¿Quién entra? ¿Ella o él?	*Who is coming in? She or he?*
No, **yo** entro ahora.	*No, I am coming in now.*

Subject pronouns are used as substitutes for nouns or noun phrases that have already been named or understood in context in order to avoid unnecessary repetition.

Carlos y Martín viajan a Perú. **Ellos** son mis hermanos.	*Carlos and Martín travel to Peru. They are my brothers.*
Mi madre trabaja aquí. **Ella** recibe un descuento.	*My mother works here. She gets a discount.*

When used as the subject in an indefinite sentence, *it* has no equivalent subject pronoun in Spanish.

Es hora de comer.	*It is time to eat.*

Now, practice what you have studied and learned about subject pronouns in Spanish.

EJERCICIO
1·1

Repaso. *Complete the sentence with the appropriate subject pronoun to replace the underlined words.*

1. Mi hermana no vive aquí. _____ vive en California.

2. Las chicas no son mexicanas, _____ son panameñas.

3. Aquí está ya el Sr. López. _____ llega temprano, como siempre.

4. ¿Quién, Carlos o Marta? _____ bajan la escalera.

5. Marisa y yo leemos siempre en la sala. _____ nos llevamos bien.

6. ¡Ana, Pedro! ¡Hola! ¡_____ pueden subir ya!

7. María y Luis son mis amigos. Por eso _____ me ayudan tanto.

8. Usted y el Sr. López pasan ahora al frente de la oficina. _____ deben esperar allí.

The present tense

There are three conjugations of verbs in Spanish with infinitives that end in **-ar**, **-er**, or **-ir**. To form the present tense, replace the infinitive ending with the appropriate personal ending:

-ar verbs:	**-o, -as, -a, -amos, -áis, -an**
-er verbs:	**-o, -es, -e, -emos, -éis, -en**
-ir verbs:	**-o, -es, -e, -imos, -ís, -en**

The following are examples of regular verbs of each conjugation in the present tense. Irregular verbs, and verbs with changes in spelling and in the stem, are reviewed later.

	gastar to spend	**vender** to sell	**abrir** to open
yo	gasto	vendo	abro
tú	gastas	vendes	abres
usted	gasta	vende	abre
él/ella	gasta	vende	abre
nosotros	gastamos	vendemos	abrimos
vosotros	gastáis	vendéis	abrís
ustedes	gastan	venden	abren
ellos/ellas	gastan	venden	abren

In the first person singular (the **yo** form), the ending is the same in all three conjugations. In -**er** and -**ir** verbs the endings are the same in the third person forms.

Luisa **come** frutas tropicales.   *Luisa eats tropical fruits.*

Pero ella **vive** en Quito.   *But she lives in Quito.*

EJERCICIO
1·2

En casa. *Complete the sentence with the appropriate form of the present tense of the verb in parentheses.*

1. Yo _____. (cantar)

2. Él _____. (escuchar)

3. Ustedes _____. (bailar)

4. Ellas _____. (descansar)

5. Nosotras _____ la cena. (preparar)

6. Tú _____ los platos. (lavar)

7. Tú no _____ tus secretos. (compartir)

8. Yo _____ en ti. (confiar)

9. Ellas _____. (decidir)

10. Ustedes _____. (responder)

11. Mi esposo _____. (entrar)

12. Nuestra hija _____ un regalo. (recibir)

13. Ustedes _____ las cifras. (sumar)

14. Nosotros _____ el total. (dividir)

15. Los niños _____ los juguetes. (romper)

16. Yo los _____ a la basura. (echar)

17. Julia _____ de dolor de cabeza. (sufrir)

18. Miguel _____ el piano. (tocar)

19. Nosotros _____ este ejercicio. (terminar)

20. Ustedes _____ ahora por fin. (descansar)

EJERCICIO
1·3

Traducción. *Use the present tense to translate each sentence. Include the subject pronoun if needed.*

1. You (*sing., fam.*) need to rest.

   _____

2. He talks, I listen.

   _____

3. She studies Chinese and Spanish, too.

   _____

4. We (*masc.*) spend too much money.

   _____

5. You (*pl., form.*) buy expensive shirts.

   _____

6. I work five days a week.

   _____

7. They (*fem.*) dance every Saturday.

   _____

8. My sister plays the piano, but I play the guitar.

   _____

Uses of the present tense

The present tense is used in many common expressions.

- ◆ Actions or situations that are going on at this moment

  ¿Hablas con tus amigos?   *Do you talk to your friends?*

- ◆ Activities and routines that take place regularly even if they are not happening at this moment

  Los domingos no **trabajo**.   *I do not work on Sundays.*

- ◆ Activities that will happen in the near future

  El próximo viernes **cocinamos** en casa.   *Next Friday we will cook at home.*

To express what is happening right now, Spanish uses the present progressive tense. The present progressive is used less frequently in Spanish than in English. Chapter 3 reviews the uses of **estar** with the present progressive.

  Estamos descansando en el sofá.   *We are resting on the sofa.*

VOCABULARIO

Below are common regular verbs of all three conjugations that you may use for the exercises that follow.

-AR VERBS		**-ER** VERBS		**-IR** VERBS	
arreglar	*to fix*	**beber**	*to drink*	**admitir**	*to admit*
conversar	*to talk*	**correr**	*to run*	**asistir**	*to attend*
cooperar	*to cooperate*	**creer**	*to believe*	**compartir**	*to share*
dedicar	*to dedicate*	**deber**	*to owe*	**cubrir**	*to cover*
desarrollar	*to develop*	**poseer**	*to own*	**describir**	*to describe*
disfrutar	*to enjoy*	**responder**	*to answer*	**existir**	*to exist*
pasar	*to spend time*	**romper**	*to break*	**permitir**	*to allow*
trabajar	*to work*	**temer**	*to fear*	**repartir**	*to distribute*
utilizar	*to use*	**vender**	*to sell*	**sufrir**	*to suffer*

EJERCICIO
1·4

En la tienda. Traducción.

1. We open the store at eight.

_____

2. You (*pl., form.*) talk to the customers.

_____

3. We answer their questions.

_____

4. You (*sing., fam.*) distribute the flyers (**folletos de publicidad**).

_____

5. You (*sing., fam.*) describe the qualities of our products.

_____

6. We work a lot here.

_____

7. You (*pl., form.*) spend a lot of time with your family.

_____

8. But I admit that I work many hours.

_____

EJERCICIO
1·5

Traducción.

I live in Tampa, Florida. Near our office there is a very popular Cuban restaurant, "Casa Manolo." My friends and I eat at this restaurant. We walk to the restaurant and read the lunch menu with the specials of the day. The waiter always describes the special dishes. He opens a bottle of mineral water for the table. Mauricio and I always eat black beans, a typical Cuban dish. A nice lunch ends with a delicious dark and sweet coffee, a Cuban coffee. After lunch we return to the office.

_____

_____

_____

_____

_____

_____

_____

_____

_____

_____

Spelling changes in the present tense

In some texts you may find verbs that undergo spelling changes grouped as irregular verbs. Some verbs have spelling changes in the **yo** form *only* to maintain the sound of the final stem consonant.

- Verbs ending in -**ncer** or -**rcer** change **c** to **z** before the -**o** ending

conve**ncer**	*to convince*	→ convenzo
eje**rcer**	*to practice as*	→ ejerzo
ve**ncer**	*to win*	→ venzo

- Verbs ending in -**rcir** change **c** to **z** before the -**o** ending

zur**cir**	*to mend*	→ zurzo

- Verbs ending in -**ger** change **g** to **j** before the -**o** ending

co**ger**	*to catch, grab*	→ cojo
enco**ger**	*to shrink*	→ encojo
esco**ger**	*to choose*	→ escojo
prote**ger**	*to protect*	→ protejo
reco**ger**	*to pick up*	→ recojo

- Verbs ending in -**gir** to change **g** to **j** before the -**o** ending

diri**gir**	*to direct*	→ dirijo
exi**gir**	*to demand*	→ exijo
fin**gir**	*to pretend*	→ finjo
sumer**gir**	*to immerse*	→ sumerjo

- Verbs ending in -**guir** change **gu** to **g** before the -**o** ending

distin**guir**	*to distinguish*	→ distingo
extin**guir**	*to extinguish*	→ extingo

EJERCICIO 1·6

Mis decisiones ecológicas. *Complete each sentence with the appropriate present tense* **yo** *form of the verb in parentheses.*

1. _____ las especies de animales. (proteger)

2. _____ a mis vecinos para ayudar al medio ambiente. (convencer)

3. _____ los derechos de los animales. (exigir)

4. _____ las botellas plásticas en mi barrio. (recoger)

5. _____ los métodos mejores para ayudar a la comunidad. (escoger)

6. _____ una profesión ecológica: biología marina. (ejercer)

7. _____ un grupo de jóvenes para recoger basura en el lago. (dirigir)

8. _____ las diferencias entre ecología y biología. (distinguir)

EJERCICIO
1·7

Y en tu caso, ¿verdadero (V) o falso (F)?

1. _____ Escojo a buenos amigos.

2. _____ Gasto mucho dinero en las tiendas.

3. _____ Zurzo mis medias.

4. _____ Saludo a mis vecinos todos los días.

5. _____ Hablo mucho por teléfono.

6. _____ Escucho música por Internet.

7. _____ Lavo mi ropa en una lavadora.

8. _____ Recojo a mis amigos en mi trabajo.

9. _____ Sufro mucho en mi trabajo.

10. _____ Discuto mis problemas con mi jefe.

11. _____ Miro programas de televisión por la noche.

12. _____ Recibo más de veinte mensajes electrónicos en mi teléfono.

13. _____ No como mucho cuando voy a un restaurante.

EJERCICIO
1·8

Mi familia. Traducción. *Use the words in the* **Vocabulario útil** *for your translation.*

VOCABULARIO ÚTIL

downtown	**el centro (de la ciudad)**
fancy	**caro, -a / lujoso, -a**
finally	**por fin**
meal	**la comida**
rarely	**casi nunca / rara vez**
team	**el equipo**
to plant	**sembrar**

My wife, Delia, works at a fancy store downtown. I help around the house. I pick up the garbage every morning. My daughter, Mariana, always cooperates with me. Today, I convince Mariana: she sews on my shirt buttons—finally. Mariana and I plant vegetables in our backyard and we work hard. I always choose organic products for our meals. Sam, my son, never pretends to be happy. He rarely wins when he plays baseball with his team. But he always demands his rights. Sam and I drink a soda and we talk about sports after the game. That is my family.

_____

_____

_____

_____

_____

_____

_____

_____

_____

_____

_____

Present tense irregular verbs

You already know that many frequently used verbs in Spanish are considered irregular. Among these are verbs that undergo a change in the last vowel of the stem.

Verbs with stem changes in the present tense

The vowel change in the stem of the present tense does not affect the personal endings, which remain the same. The stem change holds for all forms except the **nosotros/nosotras** and **vosotros/vosotras** forms.

Siempre **pienso** en mis amigos.	*I always think about my friends.*
Nosotros **preferimos** las sillas azules.	*We prefer the blue chairs.*

Stem change e → ie

The conjugations of -**ar**, -**er**, and -**ir** verbs that change the stem vowel **e** to **ie** are as follows:

pensar *to think*	**querer** *to love*	**preferir** *to prefer*
pienso	quiero	prefiero
piensas	quieres	prefieres
piensa	quiere	prefiere
pensamos	queremos	preferimos
pensáis	queréis	preferís
piensan	quieren	prefieren

VOCABULARIO

Here are some verbs with the **e** → **ie** stem change that you may use for the exercises that follow.

-**AR** VERBS		-**ER** VERBS		-**IR** VERBS	
atravesar	*to cross over*	**ascender**	*to promote*	**advertir**	*to notify, warn*
cerrar	*to close*	**defender**	*to defend*	**convertir**	*to convert*
comenzar	*to start*	**descender**	*to go down*	**divertir**	*to have fun*

confesar	to confess	encender	to light up	herir	to hurt
despertar	to wake up	encerrar	to lock in	hervir	to boil
empezar	to start	entender	to understand	mentir	to lie
fregar	to scrub	perder	to lose, miss	presentir	to sense
gobernar	to govern, rule			sentir	to feel
negar	to deny				
recomendar	to advise				
sentar	to sit				

La rutina de Julia en la casa. *Complete each sentence with the appropriate present tense **ella** form of the verb in parentheses.*

1. Todos los días, Julia_____ las escaleras. (descender)

2. Después,_____ a su esposo. (despertar)

3. Luego_____ la luz de la cocina. (encender)

4. _____ a preparar el café. (empezar)

5. También,_____ el agua para el té de su esposo. (hervir)

6. _____ los platos y las tazas. (fregar)

7. Entonces_____ el pasillo para ir a su oficina. (atravesar)

8. _____ su trabajo en la oficina en su casa. (comenzar)

9. Después_____ a su gato en una silla cerca de la computadora. (sentar)

10. Quiere silencio y_____ la puerta de la oficina. (cerrar)

Un programa de radio. *First underline the verb in parentheses that best fits the meaning of each sentence. Then fill in the appropriate present tense form of the verb.*

Modelo: Nosotros (sentar / negar) la noticia.

Nosotros_____ la noticia. (sentar / negar)

Nosotros negamos la noticia.

1. Ahora_____ el programa de noticias. (comenzar / convertir)

_____

2. La presentadora_____ a los oyentes (*listeners*). (confesar / divertir)

_____

3. Los oyentes _____ una voz agradable. (referir / sentir)

_____

4. Los oyentes comentan y _____ sus ideas. (defender / encender)

_____

5. Los anuncios _____ muchos productos naturales. (fregar / recomendar)

_____

6. A veces, _____ una canción antes de otras noticias. (empezar / perder)

_____

7. ¡Noticia de última hora! La emisora _____ una tormenta de nieve.
(advertir / querer)

_____

8. Las autoridades _____ las autopistas (*expressways*) mañana. (encerrar /
cerrar)

_____

Stem change o → ue

The conjugations of -**ar**, -**er**, and -**ir** verbs that change the stem vowel **o** to **ue** are as follows:

contar *to count, tell*	**poder** *to be able, can*	**dormir** *to sleep*
cuento	puedo	duermo
cuentas	puedes	duermes
cuenta	puede	duerme
contamos	podemos	dormimos
contáis	podéis	dormís
cuentan	pueden	duermen

VOCABULARIO

Below you find verbs with the **o** → **ue** stem change, mostly -**ar** and -**er** verbs. Use them for the
exercises that follow.

-**AR** VERBS		-**ER** VERBS		-**IR** VERBS	
almorzar	*to eat lunch*	**conmover**	*to move, to touch*	**morir**	*to die*
aprobar	*to approve*	**devolver**	*to return*		
colgar	*to hang*	**doler**	*to hurt*		
costar	*to cost*	**llover**	*to rain, pour*		
demostrar	*to prove*	**morder**	*to bite*		
encontrar	*to find*	**mover**	*to move*		

mostrar	*to show*	**oler**	*to smell*
recordar	*to remember*	**resolver**	*to solve*
rogar	*to beg*	**revolver**	*to stir*
soñar (con)	*to dream*	**volver**	*to return*
sonar	*to ring, sound*	**soler**	*to tend to*
volar	*to fly*		

The verb **oler** also adds an **h** to all forms *except* **nosotros** and **vosotros: huelo, hueles,** etc.

No **huelo** las flores.	*I do not smell the flowers.*
Vosotros **oléis** los pasteles.	*You smell the pastries.*

Note also that in the verb **jugar,** the **u** in the stem changes to **ue** in all forms *except* **nosotros** and **vosotros**.

Yo **juego** tenis los sábados.	*I play tennis every Saturday.*
Jugamos al ajedrez.	*We play chess.*

EJERCICIO
2·3

Mis amigos Bernardo y José. Traducción.

1. Bernardo and José tend to help their friends.

_____

2. When it rains, José picks me up at my office.

_____

3. Bernardo remembers my birthday every year.

_____

4. I eat lunch with José frequently.

_____

5. They play golf on Sundays.

_____

6. When I play with them, I count the points for the score (**el resultado**).

_____

7. José flies to Costa Rica every summer.

_____

8. He usually returns to Albuquerque after one week.

_____

Usa la lógica. *Write in the letter of the phrase that best completes each sentence.*

1. _____ Duerme   a. gana siempre contra sus amigos.

2. _____ Devuelve casi siempre   b. una manzana; tiene hambre.

3. _____ Cuelga la ropa   c. en el ropero de su habitación.

4. _____ Demuestra su mejor característica: d. la generosidad a su comunidad.

5. _____ Huele el perfume   e. piensa mucho y toma decisiones.

6. _____ Resuelve sus problemas porque   f. de una rosa en la terraza.

7. _____ Muerde   g. tiene buena memoria.

8. _____ Recuerda mucho,   h. en el sofá de la sala.

9. _____ Cuenta   i. los regalos de sus amigos.

10. _____ Juega todos los domingos y   j. el dinero en el banco.

Stem change e → i

The conjugation of **-ir** verbs with the **e → i** stem vowel change is as follows:

pedir *to ask for, request*

pido	pedimos
pides	pedís
pide	piden

VOCABULARIO

Now, review the list of commonly used verbs with the **e → i** stem change that may be useful for the exercises that follow:

competir	*to compete*	**medir**	*to measure*
conseguir	*to get, obtain*	**perseguir**	*to pursue, follow*
decir	*to say, tell*	**reír**	*to laugh*

despedir	*to fire*	repetir	*to repeat*
elegir	*to choose, elect*	seguir	*to follow, continue*
freír	*to fry*	servir	*to serve*
gemir	*to moan*	sonreír	*to smile*
impedir	*to avoid, prevent*	vestir	*to dress*

Some verbs in this list have additional spelling changes and a written accent.

- **Seguir, conseguir: u** follows **g** where needed to maintain the hard **g** sound: **sigues, sigue, siguen**; consigues, consigue, consiguen.

Siempre tú **sigues** las reglas de la clase.	*You always follow the class rules.*
Juan **consigue** un trabajo excelente.	*Juan gets an excellent job.*

- All forms of **reír** and **sonreír** have a written accent on the stem vowel **í**.

Mis amigos **ríen** cuando terminan su trabajo.	*My friends laugh when they finish their work.*
¿Por qué no **sonríen** los chicos?	*Why don't the children smile?*

- In addition to the stem vowel change, the **yo** form of **elegir** is **elijo**, and the **yo** form of **decir** is **digo**.

Elijo estos libros.	*I choose these books.*
No siempre **digo** la verdad.	*I do not always tell the truth.*

Vowel changes in verbs ending in -uir

For verbs ending in -**uir** not preceded by **g**, **y** is inserted after the **u**, except in the **nosotros** and **vosotros** forms.

concluir *to conclude, to finish*	
concluyo	concluimos
concluyes	concluís
concluye	concluyen

VOCABULARIO

This is a short list of commonly used verbs ending in -**uir** *not* preceded by a **g**.

construir	*to build, construct*	huir	*to flee, run away*
contribuir	*to contribute*	incluir	*to include*
destruir	*to destroy*	influir	*to influence*
distribuir	*to distribute*	sustituir	*to substitute*

En el banco. *Complete each sentence with the appropriate present tense form of the verb in parentheses.*

1. En el banco, un cliente_____ una hipoteca (*mortgage*). (conseguir)

2. La cajera (*teller*)_____ un documento de identidad (*ID card*) a los clientes. (pedir)

3. Los empleados saludan a los clientes y_____. (sonreír)

4. Todos los empleados_____ las reglas de la oficina. (seguir)

5. Un joven_____ café a los clientes. (servir)

6. Este banco_____ con otros bancos en mi barrio. (competir)

7. Al final del día, el guardia_____ un robo. (impedir)

8. El ladrón_____ en su auto. (huir)

9. ¡Qué pena! El gerente_____ a dos empleados hoy. (despedir)

10. El día de trabajo_____ a las seis de la tarde. (concluir)

Y en tu caso, ¿verdadero (V) o falso (F)?

1. _____ Gimo cuando siento dolor en una muela.

2. _____ Mido mis palabras cuando hablo con mi jefe.

3. _____ Río cuando escucho chistes.

4. _____ Visto a mi perro con un suéter cuando salimos al parque.

5. _____ Repito palabras en español en voz alta.

6. _____ Sirvo té a mis colegas en la oficina.

7. _____ Elijo a buenos candidatos en las elecciones de mi país.

8. _____ Pido sal cuando como en un restaurante.

Irregular verbs

As you have learned, many frequently used irregular verbs change their forms in different ways. With some (e.g., **ir**) all forms are irregular, in others (e.g., **tener**) only some forms change, and in many verbs only the **yo** form is irregular.

Frequently used irregular verbs

Irregular forms in the following frequently used verbs are printed in bold.

ir *to go*	oír *to hear*	ser *to be*	tener *to have*	venir *to come*
voy	oigo	soy	tengo	vengo
vas	oyes	eres	tienes	vienes
va	oye	es	tiene	viene
vamos	oímos	somos	tenemos	venimos
vais	oís	sois	tenéis	venís
van	oyen	son	tienen	vienen

Verbs that are irregular in the **yo** form only

Many verbs that end in **-cer** or **-cir** preceded by **e**, **o**, or **u** add **z** in the **yo** form only.

agradecer	*to be thankful*	agradezco
aparecer	*to appear*	aparezco
conocer	*to know*	conozco
conducir	*to drive*	conduzco
crecer	*to grow*	crezco
desaparecer	*to disappear*	desaparezco
establecer	*to establish*	establezco
merecer	*to deserve*	merezco
obedecer	*to obey*	obedezco
ofrecer	*to offer*	ofrezco
pertenecer	*to belong*	pertenezco
producir	*to produce*	produzco

Some **-er** verbs add **g** before the present tense endings.

caer	*to fall*	caigo
hacer	*to do*	hago
poner	*to put*	pongo
salir	*to leave*	salgo
traer	*to bring*	traigo
valer	*to be worth*	valgo

Other commonly used verbs also are irregular in the **yo** form only.

caber	*to fit*	quepo
dar	*to give*	doy
estar	*to be*	estoy
saber	*to know*	sé

The addition of prefixes **com-**, **des-**, **dis-**, **pro-**, **-re**, **-su**, and so on does not change the irregular forms of the verbs **hacer**, **poner**, **tener**, and **traer**.

hacer

deshacer	*to undo*	**deshago**
rehacer	*to remake*	**rehago**

poner

componer	*to compose*	**compongo**
disponer	*to arrange*	**dispongo**
proponer	*to propose*	**propongo**
reponer	*to replace*	**repongo**
suponer	*to suppose*	**supongo**

tener

contener	*to contain, hold*	**contengo**
entretener	*to distract, entertain*	**entretengo**
retener	*to keep, retain*	**retengo**
sostener	*to hold up, support*	**sostengo**

traer

atraer	*to attract*	**atraigo**
distraer	*to distract*	**distraigo**
sustraer	*to subtract*	**sustraigo**

EJERCICIO
2·7

En la oficina. *Complete each sentence with the appropriate present tense form of the verb in parentheses.*

1. Yo nunca miento, siempre_____ la verdad. (decir)

2. Marta no_____ veinte años, ¡treinta! (tener)

3. En la oficina, yo_____ mi cartera en la gaveta. (poner)

4. Yo_____ los nombres de todos los países europeos. (saber)

5. Carlos_____ mañana de Argentina. (venir)

6. Yo_____ las gracias a mis amigos. (dar)

7. Luisa_____ puertorriqueña. (ser)

8. Ahora yo_____ aquí, delante de la computadora. (estar)

9. Yo no_____ mucho dinero a la oficina. (traer)

10. Brenda y yo_____ música cuando trabajamos. (oír)

11. Pedro siempre_____ su trabajo. (hacer)

12. Pedro propone un restaurante para almorzar pero yo_____ otro. (proponer)

Preguntas personales.

1. ¿A qué hora sales de casa por la mañana?

    _____

2. ¿Conduces un auto nuevo o viejo?

    _____

3. ¿Perteneces a un partido político en tu país?

    _____

4. ¿Qué traes a casa cuando vas al mercado?

    _____

5. ¿Haces tareas en español o alemán?

    _____

6. ¿Mereces un descanso después de este ejercicio? ¿Sí o no?

    _____

Uses of the irregular verbs saber and conocer

Remember both **saber** and **conocer** are irregular in the present and both mean *to know*. However, in Spanish they are used in different contexts.

- **saber**: *to know information and facts, to know how*

Ellos saben los detalles del accidente.	*They know the details about the accident.*
Lola sabe que vivo en la Florida.	*Lola knows that I live in Florida.*
Sé tocar la guitarra.	*I know how to play the guitar.*

- **conocer**: *to be familiar with a person, a place, or a location; to meet a person*

Conozco a Juan.	*I know Juan.*
No conocemos ese museo.	*We are not familiar with that museum.*
Es un gusto conocer a su hijo.	*It is a pleasure to meet your son.*

Una conversación. ¿Conocer o saber? *Complete the following sentences using the* **yo** *form of the present tense of* **saber** *or* **conocer** *as appropriate.*

1. _____ a Sebastián, el hijo de Martina.

2. _____ dónde vive Sebastián.

3. No_____ este lugar muy bien.

4. _____ algunas tiendas excelentes aquí.

5. No_____ los nombres de las estaciones de trenes tampoco.

6. _____ que Buenos Aires es una ciudad muy cosmopolita.

7. _____ a muchas personas en México.

8. Y_____ buenas playas en ese país.

La familia y los amigos. Traducción. *Use the words in the* **Vocabulario útil** *for your translation.*

VOCABULARIO ÚTIL

around	**alrededor de, a eso de**
bye	**hasta pronto**
doorbell	**el timbre, la campana de la puerta**
health	**la salud**
healthy	**saludable**
midnight	**la medianoche**
musician	**el músico / la música**
to choose	**escoger**
twice	**dos veces**

My cousin Julia comes to my house every Friday evening. I leave my store early and I drive my car to the supermarket. I choose green vegetables, lettuce, tomatoes, and other products. I belong to an organization, "Health is life." I go to the meetings twice a month. When I get home, I put the bags in the kitchen and I start cooking quickly. The door bell rings and I open the door. I see Julia and I give her a kiss. I always offer Julia an opportunity to cook our dinner. If my neighbor Felipe hears our voices, or smells the food, he comes to my house. He has a guitar. He brings the guitar and he plays two or three songs. Around midnight I say good-bye. I am sleepy! Bye.

_____

_____

_____

_____

_____

_____

_____

_____

_____

_____

_____

Ser and estar, and adjectives

As you have learned, the verbs **ser** and **estar** are used differently according to context to communicate the meaning of the verb *to be*.

Ser and estar

The following review will help you distinguish the uses of **ser** and **estar**.

Yo **soy** muy generoso.		*I am very generous.*
Estoy en mi apartamento.		*I am in my apartment.*

ser *to be*				estar *to be*			
soy	*I am*	somos	*we are*	estoy	*I am*	estamos	*we are*
eres	*you are*	sois	*you are*	estás	*you are*	estáis	*you are*
es	*you are*	son	*you are*	está	*you are*	están	*you are*
es	*he, she is*	son	*they are*	está	*he, she is*	están	*they are*

Let's review the uses of **ser** and **estar**.

Uses of ser

Use **ser** to communicate or indicate the following:

- Origin: the place where a person or an animal was born

¿**De dónde son** tus padres?	*Where are your parents from?*
Mi caballo **es de** Kentucky.	*My horse is from Kentucky.*

- Nationality (nationalities are not capitalized in Spanish)

Vivo en Francia pero **soy** argentina.	*I live in France but I am Argentinian.*

- Profession and occupation

El Sr. Gómez **es** enfermero.	*Mr. Gómez is a nurse.*
Soy estudiante y **soy** vendedor también.	*I am a student and I am also a salesperson.*

- Characteristics of personality and attributes

    Uds. **son** concienzudos.   *You are conscientious.*

    Los perros **son** fieles a los amos.   *Dogs are loyal to their masters.*

- Description: color, size, materials of composition, etc.

    Los ojos de Alina **son** verdes.   *Alina's eyes are green.*

    La casa de mi abuela **es** grande.   *My grandmother's house is large.*

    Estos zapatos **son** de cuero.   *These are leather shoes.*

- Religious and political affiliations (adjectives that describe a religion are not capitalized in Spanish)

    Julián **es** episcopal.   *Julián is Episcopalian.*

    Mariano y su esposa **son** demócratas.   *Mariano and his wife are democrats.*

- Possession

    ¿De quién **es** esta maleta?   *Whose suitcase is this?*

- Relationships: by blood, marriage, friendship, profession, occupation

    Carlos **es** el primo de Sandra.   *Carlos is Sandra's cousin.*

    Juanita **es** la esposa de Pedro.   *Juanita is Pedro's wife.*

    El Sr. Fernández **es** mi gerente.   *Mr. Fernandez is my manager.*

    Los González **son** nuestros vecinos.   *The Gonzalezes are our neighbors.*

- Events

    La boda de Miguel **es** en la catedral. *Miguel's wedding is at the cathedral.*

    ¿Mañana **es** tu cumpleaños?   *Is your birthday tomorrow?*

- Date, time, and season (days and months are not capitalized in Spanish)

    Hoy **es** el domingo 17 de mayo.   *Today is Sunday May 17.*

    ¿Qué hora **es**?   *What time is it?*

    Es la primavera.   *This is spring.*

EJERCICIO
3·1

Usos del verbo *ser*. *Write in the letter of one of the reasons to use* **ser** *for each sentence.*

1. _____ Mis padres son de Uruguay.   a. origin

2. _____ Vivo en México pero soy cubano.   b. nationality

3. _____ Luisito es mi hermano.   c. occupation

4. _____ Nuestra gata es perezosa.   d. characteristic

5. _____ Mi esposa es dermatóloga.   e. relationship

6. _____ Esta es su oficina. f. event

7. _____ Es agradable y trabajadora. g. possession

8. _____ Mi cumpleaños es el dos de mayo.

Una rueda de prensa (press conference) **de fútbol.** *Which phrase best answers each question?*

1. _____ ¿A qué hora es? a. Manuel Blanco, mucho gusto

2. _____ ¿En qué lugar es la rueda? b. Listos, exigentes y excelentes

3. _____ ¿De dónde son los equipos? c. A las diez de la mañana

4. _____ ¿Quién es Paco? d. En el estudio de televisión

5. _____ ¿Cuándo es la temporada de partidos? e. En el otoño

6. _____ ¿Cómo son los entrenadores? f. El capitán del equipo

7. _____ ¿Cuándo es la conferencia? g. Mañana por la mañana

8. _____ ¿Y quien es Ud.? h. De varias zonas de América del Sur

Uses of estar

Use **estar** to indicate or describe the following:

♦ Location, position

Alicia **está** en la oficina.	*Alicia is in the office.*
Su oficina **está** cerca de su casa.	*Her office is near her house.*

♦ Emotional states, temporary health condition (one or more adjectives may follow **estar**)

¡Estoy feliz!	*I am happy!*
Arturo **está** enfermo hoy.	*Arturo is sick today.*

To say that someone has a happy disposition (a characteristic), use **ser** + **feliz**.

Somos felices. *We are happy.*

To express happiness as a temporary condition or phase, use **estar** + **feliz** (there may an explanation why this temporary condition exists).

Estamos felices porque hoy no tenemos que trabajar. *We are happy because today we do not have to work.*

- Results of past actions; a participle follows **estar** in the following examples (you will learn more about participles in Chapter 17), and must agree in gender and number with the subject

    Las cucarachas **están muertas**.   *The cockroaches are dead.*

    Jack **está casado** con Marcela.   *Jack is married to Marcela.*

There are many adjectives in Spanish that are actually past participles of verbs. One of the uses of the verb **estar** is to describe conditions that result from an action that is already past, which is what the participle indicates: The cockroaches are dead for some reason. Jack and Marcela got married and they are still married. Note that the participle agrees with the subject in gender and number: **cucarachas muertas** and **Jack casado**.

In Chapter 17 you will review and learn more about the uses of the participles of verbs for the compound tenses that need auxiliary verbs and participles.

- Weather

    El cielo **está nublado**.   *The sky is cloudy.*

    La temperatura **está** muy **baja**.   *The temperature is very low.*

There are many idiomatic expressions in Spanish with **estar**. Remember that idioms cannot be translated literally.

    Estoy de acuerdo contigo.   *I agree with you.*

    Estamos a punto de salir del edificio.   *We are about to leave the building.*

    Mis amigos **están de paso** aquí para ir a Cali.   *My friends are passing through here to go to Cali.*

In Chapter 10 you will review more expressions with **estar**, as well as idiomatic expressions with several other verbs.

EJERCICIO 3·3

Usos del verbo *estar*. *Write in the letter that indicates one of the uses of **estar** for each sentence.*

1. _____ ¿Dónde están ustedes hoy?   a. location, position

2. _____ Sé que están de buen humor.   b. emotional states

3. _____ La temperatura está a 35 grados.   c. temporary conditions

4. _____ La ciudad está al norte de Chicago.   d. weather

5. _____ Mi hermano y yo estamos en la cocina.   e. results of actions

6. _____ Este café está muy caliente.

7. _____ Mi carro está roto.

8. _____ Y hoy, mi mecánico está enfermo.

9. _____ Los pájaros están muertos.

10. _____ Hoy el día está muy frío.

EJERCICIO
3·4

Y en tu caso, ¿verdadero (V) o falso (F)?

1. _____ Estoy enfermo / enferma.

2. _____ Mi familia está en Chile.

3. _____ Hoy estoy feliz.

4. _____ Mis vecinos están en mi casa hoy.

5. _____ No tengo amigos, estoy solo / sola.

6. _____ No sé donde está Barcelona.

EJERCICIO
3·5

¿Ser o estar? *Complete each sentence with the correct form of the present tense of* **ser** *or* **estar** *as appropriate.*

1. Manuel _____ mi amigo.

2. Hoy, Manuel _____ enfermo.

3. ¿Ves? Rafael y Jorge no _____ aquí tampoco.

4. Juan y yo _____ en la oficina trabajando solos.

5. La oficina no _____ grande pero _____ cerca de mi casa.

6. Mi computadora _____ en malas condiciones.

7. La computadora de Manuel _____ nueva y la uso hoy.

8. Hoy _____ viernes y por eso yo _____ feliz.

Telling the time and date with ser and estar

To tell the time in Spanish you use **ser** + **la/las** + a cardinal number.

> **Es la una** de la madrugada. *It is one o'clock at night.*
> **Son las cuatro** de la tarde. *It is four o'clock in the afternoon.*

There are two ways to indicate a date.

- **estar** + **a** + cardinal number + **de** + month

¿A cuánto **estamos**?	*What is today's date?*
Estamos a 30 de abril.	*Today is April 30th.*

- **ser** + **el** + cardinal number + **de** + month

Mañana **es el 18 de abril**.	*Tomorrow is April 18.*

EJERCICIO
3·6

En español. *Use the words in the* **Vocabulario útil** *to answer each question, writing out the time given in parentheses.*

VOCABULARIO ÚTIL

a quarter past	**y cuarto**	*minutes to*	**menos**
a quarter to	**menos cuarto**	*noon*	**el mediodía**
half past	**y media**	*o'clock*	**en punto**
midnight	**la medianoche**	*P.M.*	**de la tarde, de la noche**
minutes after	**y**	*A.M.*	**de la mañana**

Modelo: ¿A qué hora empieza el concierto? (8 P.M.)

Empieza a las ocho en punto de la noche.

1. ¿A qué hora llegas a casa hoy? (4:00 A.M.)

   _____

2. ¿Qué hora es? (3:10 P.M.)

   _____

3. ¿Cuándo termina la clase de español? (9:00 A.M.)

   _____

4. ¿Cuándo empiezas a trabajar hoy? (12:00 P.M.)

   _____

5. ¿A qué hora sales para el trabajo? (8:45 A.M.)

   _____

6. ¿Cuándo preparas la cena? (6:15 P.M.)

   _____

Adjectives

In Spanish, adjectives usually follow a noun, with which they must agree in gender and number.

- Adjectives ending in **-o** and **-a** in the masculine and feminine singular, add an **-s** in the plural.

Compramos un auto barat**o**.	*We buy an inexpensive car.*
La tienda vende productos nuev**os**.	*The store sells new products.*
Mi casa es viej**a**.	*My house is old.*
Tengo toallas blanc**as**.	*I have white towels.*

- Adjectives ending in **-e** in the masculine and feminine singular add **-s** for both plurals.

¡El programa es formidabl**e**!	*The program is fantastic!*
La comida es excelent**e**.	*The food is excellent.*
Ana y Marcos son colegas agradabl**es**.	*Ana and Marcos are pleasant colleagues.*

- Adjectives ending in a consonant are the same in the masculine and feminine singular; both plurals add **-es**.

El ejercicio es muy fáci**l**.	*This exercise is very easy.*
Hago trabajo y tarea difíci**les** en casa.	*I do hard work and homework at home.*

- Adjectives that end in **-z** form the plural by changing **-z** to **-ces**.

el hombre feli**z**	*the happy man*	los hombres feli**ces**	*the happy men*
el león fero**z**	*the ferocious lion*	los leones fero**ces**	*the ferocious lions*
la mujer saga**z**	*the shrewd woman*	las mujeres saga**ces**	*the shrewd women*

An adjective may precede the noun to emphasize the quality of the adjective.

Disfruta la **buena vida**.	*Enjoy the good life.*

- Adjectives that end in a stressed vowel **-í** or **-ú** usually add **-es** to form the plural.

Una familia **iraní** vive aquí.	*An Iranian family lives here.*
Las recetas **iraníes** son sabrosas.	*The Iranian recipes are delicious.*

- Some adjectives may drop the accent mark in order to keep the stressed vowel.

Alex es **francés**. Ellas son **francesas**.	*Alex is French. They are French.*
Louis es **inglés y** Ana es **inglesa** también.	*Louis is English and Ana is English, too.*
Juan es **cortés**. Pedro y Pablo también son **corteses**.	*Juan is courteous. Pedro and Pablo are courteous, too.*

EJERCICIO 3·7

En el zoológico. *Complete each sentence with the appropriate form of the adjectives in parentheses.*

1. Manuel visita un zoológico _____ y _____.
(interesante, fantástico)

2. En unas jaulas (*cage*) _____ hay leones _____.
(grande, feroz)

3. Los osos panda comen plantas _____ y _____.
(exótico, fresco)

4. El clima de San Diego es _____, no _____.
(templado, frío)

5. El zoológico es _____: protege especies _____
(especial, raro).

6. Hay plantas _____ y _____. (medicinal, tóxica)

EJERCICIO 3·8

Lectura. *Read the paragraph below, then underline all the adjectives.*

Felicia es joven, alta y tiene ojos negros y grandes. Ella es madrileña. Es elegante y toca música clásica con la guitarra. Fernando, su hermano, es alegre y es pianista. Él mezcla el jazz norteamericano con el flamenco andaluz. Felicia y Fernando viven en una casa antigua pero agradable. En el jardín hay flores blancas, amarillas y rojas. Fernando es dormilón. Su madre, Mercedes, dice que es haragán pero él practica el piano por largas horas. Fernando está cansado ahora y escucha música popular de varios países.

EJERCICIO 3·9

Read the paragraph in Ejercicio 3-8 again. Then answer the following questions.

1. ¿Qué adjetivo indica el origen de Felicia?

_____

2. ¿Qué adjetivos aparecen para describir a Felicia físicamente?

_____

3. ¿Cuál es la profesión de Fernando?

_____

4. Escribe una lista de los adjetivos que describen a Fernando.

_____

5. ¿Qué adjetivos describen la casa donde viven Fernando y su hermana?

_____

Adjectives with shortened forms

A few adjectives drop the final –o when they are preceded by a singular masculine noun.

alguno	*some*	algún	ninguno	*no, not any*	ningún
bueno	*good*	buen	primero	*first*	primer
malo	*bad*	mal	tercero	*third*	tercer

Ali recibirá **algún mensaje** hoy.   *Ali will receive some messages today.*
Su esposo es un **buen electricista**.   *Her husband is a good electrician.*
Ningún estudiante llega temprano aquí. *No students arrive here early.*

**EJERCICIO
3·10**

Traducción.

1. I am a good person.

_____

2. I (*masc.*) live in Miami and I am Mexican.

_____

3. I am pleasant and courteous.

_____

4. My apartment is on the first floor.

_____

5. I do have some problems with my neighbor.

_____

6. She is picky (**quisquilloso**) and gossipy.

_____

7. She is a bad influence in my building.

_____

8. She is always in a bad mood.

_____

Adjectives with ser and estar

Remember that several adjectives have different meanings in Spanish depending on whether they are used with **ser** or with **estar**.

ser + aburrido	_to be boring_		**estar + aburrido**	_to be bored_
ser + bueno	_to be good_		**estar + bueno**	_to be in good condition_
ser + libre	_to be free_		**estar + libre**	_to be available_
ser + listo	_to be smart_		**estar + listo**	_to be ready_
ser + malo	_to be bad_		**estar + malo**	_to be ill, in bad condition_
ser + maduro	_to be mature_		**estar + maduro**	_to be ripe_
ser + rico	_to be rich_		**estar + rico**	_to be tasty_
ser + seguro	_to be safe_		**estar + seguro**	_to be certain, sure_
ser + viejo	_to be old_		**estar + viejo**	_to look old_
ser + vivo	_to be sharp_		**estar + vivo**	_to be alive_

EJERCICIO
3·11

¿Ser o estar? _Complete each sentence with the correct form of the present tense of_ **ser** _or_ **estar**, _as appropriate._

1. Los hermanos Mestre _____ ricos.

2. Luis tiene 15 años pero _____ maduro para su edad.

3. Hoy Miguel _____ malo. Tiene fiebre.

4. Ellos dos casi siempre _____ aburridos en la casa.

5. Yo _____ seguro que son de una buena familia.

6. Ahora, yo _____ listo para ir a su casa.

7. Los abuelos _____ viejos pero son cómicos.

8. El abuelo _____ vivo y gana cuando juega dominó.

9. La abuela siempre _____ libre para ir al cine.

10. En su casa, siempre la merienda _____ rica.

Estar and the present progressive

The present progressive is used to express ongoing actions—what is happening at this very moment. To form the present progressive, use the present tense of **estar** + the present participle of the main verb. It is used less frequently in Spanish than in English.

Están lavando mi ropa.	*They are washing my clothes.*
Mis padres **están comiendo** ahora.	*My parents are eating now.*

Most present participles are regular in Spanish. Remember that -**er** and -**ir** verbs share the same present participle endings. The present participle remains constant: it does not change with number or gender.

	INFINITIVE	STEM + ENDING	PRESENT PARTICIPLE
-**ar** verbs	**cantar**	**cant** + -**ando**	→ **cantando**
-**er** verbs	**vender**	**vend** + -**iendo**	→ **vendiendo**
-**ir** verbs	**vivir**	**viv** + -**iendo**	→ **viviendo**

You may want to review the -**ir** stem-changing verbs in Chapter 2 to understand the irregular forms of the present participles of these verbs.

INFINITIVE	**YO** FORM	STEM CHANGE	PRESENT PARTICIPLE
mentir	**miento**	e → i	**mintiendo**
pedir	**pido**	e → i	**pidiendo**
dormir	**duermo**	o → u	**durmiendo**

For -**er** and -**ir** verbs with stems that end in a vowel, **y** is added between the stem and the participle ending: **leer** → **leyendo**.

VOCABULARIO

The following are frequently used -**er** and -**ir** verbs with present participles that end in -**yendo**.

atraer	*to attract*	**atrayendo**	**construir**	*to build*	**construyendo**
caer	*to fall*	**cayendo**	**destruir**	*to destroy*	**destruyendo**
creer	*to believe*	**creyendo**	**huir**	*to flee*	**huyendo**
leer	*to read*	**leyendo**	**ir**	*to go*	**yendo**
sustraer	*to remove*	**sustrayendo**	**oír**	*to hear*	**oyendo**
traer	*to bring*	**trayendo**			

¿Qué están haciendo ahora mismo? *Underline the present tense form in each sentence. Then rewrite the sentence using the appropriate present progressive form.*

Modelo: Marisa <u>compra</u> una blusa.

Marisa está comprando una blusa.

1. Ana trae una camisa a la cajera.

_____

2. La cajera mira la etiqueta y el precio.

_____

3. Juan ayuda a una clienta.

_____

4. Un niño llora y pide agua.

_____

5. La hermanita duerme en un coche.

_____

6. Un chico lee un mensaje de texto en su teléfono.

_____

7. Un cliente busca una corbata roja.

_____

8. El gerente sale de su oficina.

_____

9. La secretaria cierra la puerta.

_____

10. Dos jóvenes entran al elevador.

_____

11. Dos chicos salen de la tienda.

_____

12. Yo voy a la casa de Marcos ahora.

_____

The near future, nouns, and articles

As previously observed, the present tense is used to indicate actions or situations that are going on at this moment, activities and routines that take place regularly, and actions that will take place in the near future. You may want to review present tense verbs in Chapter 1.

The present and the near future

Spanish tends to use the present tense rather than the future tense for actions that will occur within a short time. There are two ways to do this.

- The present tense plus adverbs or adverbial phrases that indicate when the action will take place

    El próximo lunes regresamos.   *Next Monday we will go back.*

- The verb **ir** (*to go*) + **a** + the infinitive, as in English you could say *I am going to*. All present tense forms of **ir** are irregular.

ir *to go*	
voy	**vamos**
vas	**vais**
va	**van**

Voy a ayudar a mi tía en su oficina.   *I am going to help my aunt in her office.*
Mis amigos van a viajar mañana.   *My friends are going to travel tomorrow.*

VOCABULARIO

These are some of the adverbial expressions that pinpoint the time when an action will take place in the near future.

el año que viene	*next year*	**mañana**	*tomorrow*
el mes que viene	*next month*	**mañana por la mañana**	*tomorrow morning*
esta noche	*tonight*	**mañana por la noche**	*tomorrow night*
esta tarde	*this afternoon*	**mañana por la tarde**	*tomorrow afternoon*
la semana que viene	*next week*	**más tarde**	*later on*
la semana siguiente	*the following week*	**pasado mañana**	*the day after tomorrow*

Traducción.

1. Tomorrow morning we are going to visit a museum in Madrid.

   _____

2. Later I am going to walk around the city.

   _____

3. Tomorrow afternoon Laurita is going to see her friends from Barcelona.

   _____

4. Next week Laurita and I will travel to Seville.

   _____

5. The following week you and Laura (*pl., fam.*) will return to California.

   _____

6. My parents are going to move from Los Angeles to Miami next year.

   _____

Y en tu caso, ¿verdadero (V) o falso (F)?

1. _____ El año que viene voy a estudiar alemán.

2. _____ Voy a celebrar mi cumpleaños con mis padres.

3. _____ Este fin de semana voy a ir de vacaciones.

4. _____ El próximo verano voy a graduarme de una universidad.

5. _____ Mañana vamos al cine mi novio/novia y yo.

6. _____ Voy a ir a un restaurante mexicano esta noche.

7. _____ Pasado mañana voy a jugar basquetbol.

8. _____ Mañana por la noche voy a bailar en una discoteca.

9. _____ Voy a tomar un autobús para regresar a mi casa esta semana.

10. _____ Voy a terminar estos ejercicios más tarde.

Nouns

The gender of most nouns can be determined by the ending.

Masculine nouns

A singular noun that ends in **-o** is usually masculine.

el chic**o**	*boy*	el banc**o**	*bank*
el pájar**o**	*bird*	el plat**o**	*dish*

Other nouns that are usually masculine end in **-aje**, **-és**, **-l**, **-ma**, **-or**, and **-s**.

-aje	el equip**aje**	*luggage*	el person**aje**	*character*
-és	el franc**és**	*French*	el ingl**és**	*English*
-l	el carte**l**	*sign*	el paste**l**	*pie, dessert*
-ma	el cli**ma**	*weather*	el progra**ma**	*program*
	el fantas**ma**	*ghost*	el siste**ma**	*system*
	el proble**ma**	*problem*	el te**ma**	*theme*
-or	el cal**or**	*heat*	el dol**or**	*pain*
	el rum**or**	*rumor*		
-s	el abrelata**s**	*can opener*	el parabrisa**s**	*windshield*
	el lavaplato**s**	*dishwasher*	el paragua**s**	*umbrella*

Some common nouns are exceptions to these rules.

la flo**r**	*the flower*	la pie**l**	*the skin*

Feminine nouns

Most nouns that end in **-a** are feminine (but note above the masculine nouns that end in **-ma**).

la espos**a**	*wife*	la gat**a**	*cat*	la pelot**a**	*ball*

Other endings that indicate a noun is likely to be feminine are **-dad**, **-tad**, **-ción/-sión**, **-eza**, **-sis**, and **-umbre**.

-dad	la honesti**dad**	*honesty*	la sinceri**dad**	*sincerity*
-tad	la liber**tad**	*freedom, liberty*	la ciu**dad**	*city*
-ción/sión	la can**ción**	*the song*	la direc**ción**	*address, direction*
	la ilu**sión**	*the illusion*	la pa**sión**	*passion*
-eza	la pobr**eza**	*poverty*	la trist**eza**	*sadness*
-sis	la cri**sis**	*crisis*	la do**sis**	*dose*
-umbre	la cost**umbre**	*habit, tradition*	la c**umbre**	*summit*

There are some exceptions.

el mapa	*the map*	**el planeta**	*the planet*	**el sofá**	*the sofa*

Nouns that describe an occupation or profession may have the same form in both masculine and feminine. The article indicates the gender.

el/la cantante	*the singer*	el/la líder	*the leader*
el/la representante	*the representative*	el/la mánager	*the manager*
el/la dibujante	*the draftsman*	el/la conserje	*the custodian, the receptionist*

EJERCICIO
4·3

Sustantivos. *Are the following nouns masculine (Y) or not (N)?*

1. _____ casa
2. _____ mensaje
3. _____ cama
4. _____ profesora
5. _____ televisor
6. _____ mantel
7. _____ tristeza
8. _____ taza
9. _____ niño
10. _____ dirección

11. _____ diagrama
12. _____ canción
13. _____ clima
14. _____ delantal
15. _____ dilema
16. _____ tema
17. _____ exposición
18. _____ calor
19. _____ libertad
20. _____ sección

Plural of nouns

The guidelines for forming the plural of nouns in Spanish are as follows.

♦ Nouns that end in a vowel add **-s** for the plural; nouns that end in a consonant add **-es**.

la autora	*the author*	**las autoras**
el violín	*the violin*	**los violines**

Use the masculine plural form for masculine and feminine nouns grouped together:

Marta y su amigo son **autores** de música.	*Marta and her friend are composers.*
Mario y Julia son **hermanos**.	*Mario and Julia are siblings.*

- Singular nouns that end in a stressed vowel **-í** or **-ú** usually add either **-es** or **-s** in the plural.

la marroquí	*the Moroccan*	las marroquíes, las marroquís
el bisturí	*the scalpel*	los bisturíes, los bisturís
el men**ú**	*the menu*	los men**ús**

In the plural, singular nouns that end in **-z** change the **-z** to **-ces**.

| el lá**piz** | *the pencil* → los lá**pices** |

Written accents may be dropped in the plurals of nouns with singular forms that end in **-ús** and **-ón** as they are no longer necessary to indicate a stressed vowel.

el autob**ús**	*the bus* → los autob**uses**
la raz**ón**	*the reason* → las raz**ones**
la estaci**ón**	*the season, station* → las estac**iones**

EJERCICIO
4·4

Traducción.

1. The Spanish language is very popular now in the United States.

_____

2. The papers on my desk are old.

_____

3. This trip is fantastic!

_____

4. The chairs on the terrace are comfortable.

_____

5. The financial (**financiera**) crisis affects many people.

_____

6. What is the theme of this newspaper article?

_____

7. Chocolates are a temptation!

_____

8. My fear is real: I hate roaches and mosquitoes!

_____

9. Sometimes unhappiness is a problem.

_____

10. Some habits are very weird.

_____

Articles

Definite and indefinite articles precede nouns, with which they must agree in number and gender.

The definite article

	MASCULINE		FEMININE	
SINGULAR	**el** niño	_the boy_	**la** esposa	_the wife_
PLURAL	**los** niños	_the boys_	**las** esposas	_the wives_

A definite article that follows the prepositions **a** or **de** contracts to **al** or **del**.

- **a + el → al**

    David vive **al** norte de Toledo.   _David lives to the north of Toledo._

- **de + el → del**

    Ana viene **del** sur de la ciudad.   _Ana comes from the south of the city._

An abstract noun that is the subject of a sentence takes the definite article.

    El humor mejora la salud.   _Humor improves your health._

Singular feminine nouns that begin with a stressed vowel **a-** or **ha-** take the article **el**.

    Vemos **el agua** y **el águila** aquí.   _We see the water and an eagle here._
    Uso **el hacha** para cortar el árbol.   _I use the ax to cut the tree._

When an adjective is used as a noun, the article is the invariable neuter **lo**.

    Aquí tenemos **lo bueno** y **lo malo**.   _Here we have the good and the bad._

Some nouns can take either a feminine or a masculine article; their meanings are different.

    Vemos **el cometa** con un telescopio.   _We see the comet with a telescope._
    Marcos lleva **la cometa** al parque.   _Marcos takes the kite to the park._
    El humor es **la cura** para la tristeza.   _Humor is the cure for sadness._
    En la iglesia está **el cura** Mateo.   _The priest Mateo is in the church._

The indefinite article

The indefinite article is formed as follows.

	MASCULINE		FEMININE	
SINGULAR	**un** mono	*monkey*	**una** señora	*lady*
PLURAL	**unos** monos	*monkeys*	**unas** señoras	*ladies*

In Spanish, indefinite articles are not used before nouns that indicate origin or profession, except when they are followed by an adjective.

Martina es **chilena**.	*Martina is a Chilean.*
Ella es **dentista**.	*She is a dentist.*
Julio es **un artista exitoso**.	*Julio is a successful artist.*

EJERCICIO 4·5

Práctica. *Supply the appropriate definite article for each of the following nouns.*

1. _____ árbol
2. _____ estrella
3. _____ astro
4. _____ estación
5. _____ telescopio

6. _____ luz
7. _____ satélite
8. _____ planeta
9. _____ espacio
10. _____ científico

11. _____ viaje
12. _____ programa
13. _____ astrónomo
14. _____ histeria
15. _____ meteoro

EJERCICIO 4·6

El idealismo. Traducción. *Use the words in the* **Vocabulario útil** *for your translation.*

VOCABULARIO ÚTIL

ambition	**la ambición**
craziness	**la locura**
defeat	**derrotar, vencer**
community	**la comunidad**
generosity	**la generosidad**
ignorance	**la ignorancia**
lie	**la mentira**
solve	**resolver** (*o > ue*)
truth	**la verdad**

1. What craziness! Now it is hard to tell the truth.

   _____

2. A lie is a horrible thing!

   _____

3. Ambition in Spanish means a wish (*deseo*) to be rich.

   _____

4. Generosity helps a community.

   _____

5. Ignorance does not solve a problem.

   _____

6. We are going to defeat poverty and sadness!

   _____

Los plurales. *Change the following into the plural.*

1. un francés   _____
2. un arroz   _____
3. un boletín   _____
4. una vez   _____
5. una orden   _____
6. un sillón   _____
7. una estación   _____
8. un olor (*odor*)   _____
9. un águila   _____

Esteban en la universidad. *Singular or plural? Complete the following sentences with the appropriate form of the indefinite article and the noun in parentheses.*

1. Esteban necesita _____ para estudiar en la universidad. (computadora)

2. Él compra _____ nuevos para sentarse y leer. (sillón)

3. La tía Ana le regala _____ para ver los programas educativos. (televisor)

4. La familia tiene _____ peculiares: una fiesta para el inicio del año escolar. (costumbre)

5. Esteban tiene _____: ¿comprar toallas grandes o pequeñas? (dilema)

6. Esteban escribe _____ en su libreta para no olvidar los objetos necesarios. (notas)

7. Esteban usa _____ corto para ir a clases en la universidad. (camino)

8. Está feliz. Canta _____ alegres cuando va a clase. (canción)

Preguntas personales. *Answer the following questions in complete sentences.*

1. ¿Tienes un telescopio para observar los cometas?

   _____

2. ¿Cuál es tu cura para ser feliz?

   _____

3. Tus vecinos, ¿tienen costumbres raras? Explica.

   _____

4. ¿Tienes amigos que son chilenos, españoles o de otros países?

   _____

5. ¿Conoces a un artista o a un cantante famoso?

   _____

6. ¿Usas los autobuses públicos para tu transportación todos los días?

   _____

7. ¿Tienes un problema con tus amigos?

   _____

8. ¿Cuántas veces vas al estadio para ver un partido de fútbol americano?

   _____

Adverbs and comparisons

Previously you have seen adverbs and adverbial phrases and how to use them in Spanish. As you develop confidence as a language learner, you will find you use these expressions more frequently.

Adverbs

An adverb modifies or complements the meaning of adjectives, other adverbs, verbs, and phrases. You may know some of these frequently used adverbs that indicate manner, place, or time, affirmation, denial, doubt, exclusion, etc.

VOCABULARIO

acaso	*maybe*	**mientras**	*while*
además	*furthermore*	**no**	*no*
adentro	*inside*	**nunca**	*never*
afuera	*outside*	**siempre**	*always*
ahora	*now*	**tampoco**	*either, neither*
cerca	*close, near*	**tan**	*so*
inclusive	*inclusive*	**ya**	*already*
lejos	*far*		

Siempre consumo vegetales frescos.	*I always eat fresh vegetables.*
Desde lunes a sábado, **inclusive**.	*From Monday to Saturday inclusive.*
Acaso no los voy a comer el domingo.	*Maybe I will not eat them on Sunday.*

Adverbs and their placement

In Spanish, an adverb usually follows the verb it modifies, although it may be placed at the beginning of a sentence among other places:

La ayudante trabaja **siempre** por la mañana.	*The assistant always works in the morning.*
Vivimos **lejos** de la ciudad.	*We live far from the city.*

El paciente camina **lentamente** por el pasillo.	The patient walks slowly in the hallway.
El farmacéutico lee las recetas **fácilmente**.	The pharmacist reads the prescription easily.
Felizmente Melisa no tiene caries.	Luckily, Melisa has no cavities.

- Adverbs that modify an adjective precede the adjective.

| Julián está **muy** enfermo hoy. | Julián is very sick today. |

- Adverbs that end in **-mente** (equivalent to -*ly* in English) may be placed at the beginning of a sentence.

| **Afortunadamente**, la enfermera trae un bastón. | Fortunately the nurse brings a cane. |

Adverbs are formed by attaching **-mente** to the feminine adjective.

| **peligrosa** + **-mente** → **peligrosamente** | *dangerously* |
| un individuo armado **peligrosamente** | *a dangerously armed individual* |

Adjectives that are the same in both masculine and feminine also add **-mente**.

| **atroz** | *atrocious* | **atrozmente** | *atrociously* |
| **fácil** | *easy* | **fácilmente** | *easily* |

Adverbs maintain any accent in the original adjective.

| **hábil** | *skillful* | **hábilmente** | *skillfully* |
| **difícil** | *difficult* | **difícilmente** | *with difficulty* |

If a sentence or phrase has two or more consecutive adverbs that end in **-mente**, a comma will usually be used to separate them; only the last one will add the suffix **-mente**.

| Ali habla **rápida**, **clara** y **elegantemente**. | *Ali speaks quickly, clearly, and elegantly.* |
| Ana toca el piano **hábil** y **delicadamente**. | *Ana plays the guitar skillfully and softly.* |

EJERCICIO
5·1

Los adverbios. *Form an adverb with* -**mente** *for each of the following adjectives.*

1. deprimente _____

2. tranquilo _____

3. preocupado _____

4. ansioso _____

5. triste _____

6. seguro _____

7. hábil   _____

8. feliz   _____

9. sensible   _____

10. orgulloso   _____

11. emocionado   _____

12. tímido   _____

13. agradable   _____

14. sentimental   _____

15. amable   _____

Las actitudes mentales. *Complete each sentence with one of the following adverbs, as appropriate.*

dolorosamente   moderadamente   positivamente

sinceramente   sarcásticamente   tímidamente

1. No se siente seguro, habla _____.

2. No es negativo, responde _____.

3. Mide (*to measure*) sus palabras, contesta _____.

4. Sus palabras son crueles, habla _____.

5. Su salud es preocupante, se manifiesta _____.

6. Es franco, habla _____.

Adjectives as adverbs

Some adjectives can also function as adverbs. As you see in the following examples, **rápido** is placed after a verb, **reacciona**; the next example **fácil** modifies the verb **convence**.

Marcia es lista y reacciona **rápido**.   *Marcia is smart and she reacts quickly.*
Convence a los clientes **fácil**.   *She convinces her clients easily.*

The following are commonly used adjectives that function as adverbs.

algo	somewhat	**igual**	the same
alto	loudly	**justo**	exactly
bajo	softly	**mal**	badly, poorly
barato	cheaply	**mucho**	a lot
bastante	sufficiently	**poco**	very little
claro	clearly	**rápido**	fast
fácil	easily	**regular**	fair, medium
fuerte	strongly	**suave**	softly

EJERCICIO
5·3

Lectura. *First read the paragraph below. Then underline each adverb.*

En esta tienda hay muchos productos naturales. Venden mucho y barato. Los dependientes hablan claro y explican muchos detalles cuando un cliente hace algunas preguntas. No hablan alto. Contestan las preguntas bastante claras y dan sugerencias rápido a los clientes. Distribuyen justo la información necesaria. ¿Te sientes algo cansado? Venden muchas vitaminas y no te vas a sentir igual si las tomas todos los días. ¿Duermes mal? Solución fácil: diariamente tomas un té de valeriana, una yerba saludable. ¿Para bajar de peso? Caminar dos millas todas las mañanas. Seguramente vas a usar estos productos naturales y hacer ejercicios regularmente.

EJERCICIO
5·4

Read the paragraph in Ejercicio 5-3 again. Then answer the following questions.

1. ¿Qué adverbios indican por qué venden muchos productos?

   _____

2. Escribe los dos adverbios que indican la manera en que hablan los dependientes a los clientes.

   _____

3. Escribe los adverbios que aparecen en las dos primeras preguntas del párrafo.

   _____

4. Escribe las formas que terminan en -**mente** de los adverbios **claro**, **alto**, **rápido**, **justo**, **igual**, **mal** y **fácil** que aparecen en el párrafo.

   _____

Adverbial phrases

Adverbial phrases are used in both English and Spanish, although in English it is more common to use one-word adverbs. In order to translate one-word English adverbs into Spanish, adverbial phrases are sometimes needed.

Llega **a escondidas**.	*He arrives covertly.*
Dentro de poco va a llover.	*It's going to rain shortly.*

Adverbial phrases can be formed from several prepositions and with different constructions.

- preposition + noun

a bordo	*on board*	**de golpe**	*suddenly*
a continuación	*right afterward*	**de memoria**	*by heart*
a cuentagotas	*stingily*	**de puntillas**	*on tiptoe*
a pie	*on foot*	**en cambio**	*on the other hand*
a regañadientes	*unwillingly*	**por fin**	*finally*
ante todo	*first and foremost*	**por suerte**	*luckily*
con frecuencia	*frequently*	**sin reserva**	*openly*

Felipe hace su trabajo **a regañadientes**.	*Felipe does his work unwillingly.*
Con frecuencia, hablamos **sin reserva**.	*Frequently we talk openly.*

- preposition + article + noun

a la derecha	*to the right*	**al fin**	*finally*
a la izquierda	*to the left*	**por lo general**	*generally*

Mi casa está **a la derecha** de la tienda.	*My home is at the right of the store.*
Al fin ya sabemos la verdad.	*Finally, we know the truth.*

- preposition + adjective

a menudo	*frequently*	**por cierto**	*by the way, certainly*
de nuevo	*again, anew*	**por consiguiente**	*consequently*
de pronto	*all of a sudden*	**por supuesto**	*of course*
en particular	*particularly*		

¿Tomas té **a menudo**?	*Do you drink tea frequently?*
Por cierto, el té verde tiene antioxidantes.	*By the way, green tea has antioxidants.*

- preposition + adjective + noun

de buena gana	*willingly*	**en voz alta**	*loudly*
de mala gana	*unwillingly*	**en voz baja**	*softly*

Hago ejercicios de pesas de **mala gana**.	*I work out with weights unwillingly.*

- preposition + adverb

de frente	*head-on*
de pronto	*suddenly*

De pronto Elena sale de la casa.   *Suddenly, Elena leaves the house.*

- preposition + article + a form of a verb

al amanecer	*at daybreak, at dawn*
al anochecer	*at nightfall*
al atardecer	*at dusk*

Al anochecer veo los programas   *At nightfall I watch the news*
   de noticias.   *programs.*

Adverbial phrases may seem similar in English and Spanish, but use different prepositions.

El piloto ya está **a bordo**.	*The pilot is already on board.*
Los chicos vienen **a caballo**.	*The boys come on horseback.*

EJERCICIO
5·5

Así es Julio. *Write in the letter of the adverbial phrase that best completes each sentence.*

1. _____ Sabe el poema y recita el poema   a. a pie.

2. _____ Hace sus quehaceres en casa   b. a cuentagotas.

3. _____ Es avaro y paga sus deudas   c. con frecuencia.

4. _____ Dice sus opiniones abiertamente,   d. a regañadientes.

5. _____ Llega temprano al trabajo   e. de memoria.

6. _____ Para ahorrar dinero come papas   f. sin reserva.

7. _____ Vive cerca y va a su oficina   g. a menudo.

EJERCICIO
5·6

Traducción.

1. For the first time I am going to a classical guitar concert with my friend Pedro.

_____

2. I'm going unwillingly. I do not understand classical music.

_____

3. Suddenly, I listen to the guitarist in the theater with passion.

   _____

4. I know the lyrics (**la letra**) by heart and I sing it softly.

   _____

5. Finally I know that classical music is not always boring.

   _____

EJERCICIO
5·7

Adverbios. *First write down the adjective that corresponds to each phrase. Then form the related adverb that ends in* **-mente**.

Modelo: con sinceridad

sincero, sinceramente

1. con cortesía   _____
2. con elegancia   _____
3. con alegría   _____
4. con velocidad   _____
5. con intensidad   _____
6. de nuevo   _____
7. de verdad   _____
8. en general   _____
9. por desgracia   _____
10. sin duda   _____

Comparatives of adjectives and adverbs

In Spanish there are specific ways to express comparisons.

To express equality

- **tan** + adjective + **como**

     El mango es **tan saludable como** la manzana.   *Mangoes are as healthy as apples.*

- **tan** + adverb + **como**

     Eli nos trata **tan amablemente como** su papá.   *Eli treats us as kindly as her father.*

- **tanto, -os, -as, -os** + noun + **como**

  Paco nada **tantas millas como Arturo**.   *Paco swims as many miles as Arturo.*

- pronoun **tanto, -os, -as, -os** + **como**

  Felipe tiene **tantos como** yo.   *Felipe has as many as I have.*

To express a lesser degree of quality

- **menos** + adjective + **que**

  Mi vida es **menos interesante que** la tuya.   *My life is less interesting than yours.*

- **menos** + adverb + **que**

  Luisa camina **menos rápido que** yo.   *Luisa walks less quickly than I.*

To express a greater degree of quality

- **más** + adjective + **que**

  Sol es **más inteligente que** su esposo.   *Sol is smarter than her husband.*

- **más** + adverb + **que**

  Ese tren va **más lento que** el nuestro.   *That train is running slower than ours.*

EJERCICIO
5·8

Las comparaciones. *Using the appropriate form of the present tense of the verb* **ser**, *write complete sentences to show comparison.*

Modelo: Los osos / tan / agresivo / los leones

          Los osos son tan agresivos como los leones.

1. La geografía no /menos / interesante / la historia

   _____

2. La ciudad San Diego / tan / agradable / la ciudad Santa Ana

   _____

3. Las frutas tropicales no / más / barato / las frutas de California

   _____

4. El río Grande / menos / caudaloso / el Mississippi

   _____

5. Las ciudades del sur de los Estados Unidos / más / antiguo / las ciudades del norte

_____

6. Las carreteras / menos / ancho / las autopistas de peaje (*turnpikes*)

_____

7. Las personas del sur de los EE.UU. / tan / amable / las personas del oeste del país

_____

8. Las montañas Rocosas / más / impresionante / las montañas del sureste

_____

Irregular comparatives

The adjectives **bueno**, **malo**, **grande**, and **pequeño** form their comparatives and superlatives irregularly.

bueno, -a, -os, -as *good*	mejor, -es *better*	el/la mejor, los/las mejores *the best*
malo, -a, -os, -as *bad*	peor *worse*	el/la peor, los/las peores *the worst*
grande, -es *big*	mayor, -es *more, older*	el/la mayor, los/las mayores *most, the oldest*
pequeño, -a, -os, -as *small*	menor, -es *lesser, younger*	el/la menor, los/las menores *the least, the youngest*

Menor and **mayor** are usually placed after and **mejor** before the noun:

El **hermano menor** es Juan.	*The youngest brother is Juan.*
La **hermana mayor** de Luisita es Ana.	*The older sister of Luisita is Ana.*
Don Rafael fue mi **mejor profesor**.	*Don Rafael was my best professor.*

Comparisons and superlatives

A superlative is used to indicate the greatest level of a quality. To form the superlative

- indefinite article + noun + **más** + adjective

    Elena es **la atleta más fuerte** en su grupo.   *Elena is the strongest athlete in her group.*

- indefinite article + noun + **más** + adjective + **de**

    El arroz es **el plato más barato de** todos.   *Rice is the cheapest dish of all.*

Preguntas personales.

1. ¿Quién es el mayor de tus amigos?

   _____

2. ¿Cuál es la peor de tus costumbres?

   _____

3. ¿Cuál es el problema más grande ahora para ti?

   _____

4. ¿Quién es el/la mejor cantante en tu opinión?

   _____

5. ¿Cuál es el peor equipo de fútbol americano?

   _____

6. En tu opinión, ¿quiénes son los mejores grupos de cantantes latinos?

   _____

7. ¿Quién es el jugador más fuerte de tu equipo preferido?

   _____

EJERCICIO
5·10

La salud. Traducción. *Use the words in the* **Vocabulario útil** *for your translation.*

VOCABULARIO ÚTIL

anesthetic	**la anestesia**	*hygienist*	**la higienista**
buzzing	**el zumbido**	*molar*	**la muela**
cavity	**la caries**	*policy*	**la póliza**
crown	**la corona**	*to comfort*	**consolar, reconfortar**
dental insurance	**el seguro dental**	*to faint*	**desmayarse**
drill	**el taladro**	*toothache*	**el dolor de muela**
filling	**el empaste**	*x-ray*	**rayos x**

I go to my dentist twice a year. Dr. Salazar is pleasant. The hygienist cleans my teeth carefully and gently. She takes x-rays every two years. Now I have two cavities in one molar and I need two fillings. I do not have any toothache, but I need a crown, too. Luckily, I have a dental insurance policy. Dr. Salazar says that I do not need anesthetic for my crown. My worst problem is that I faint when I hear the buzzing of the drill. I need my best friend here! Unfortunately, I am a coward!

_____

_____

_____

_____

_____

_____

_____

_____

_____

_____

Gustar and verbs like gustar

You probably have used the verb **gustar** in Spanish to express what you like or dislike. Let's review how to use the verb **gustar**.

Me gusta la música mexicana.	*I like Mexican music.*
No me gustan los platos picantes.	*I do not like spicy dishes.*

Gustar, and verbs like it, are used in the third person singular and plural *only*, and are preceded by an indirect object pronoun. That is, the subject is a person, an animal, or an item that is pleasing to the indirect object.

SPANISH	ENGLISH
indirect object + **gustar** + subject	subject + *to like* + direct object
Me **gusta** el programa.	*I like the program.*

The translation of **gustar** is *to like, to please.* In Spanish the word order is not rigid—the preceding example could be changed to **El programa me gusta** (*The program is pleasing to me*). Placing the subject first in a sentence with **gustar** stresses what it is that is pleasing to the indirect object **me** (*me*)—**el programa**. Note that any negative words precede the indirect pronoun.

No me gustan los colores claros.	*I do not like light colors.*
No les gusta una paella con alcachofas.	*They do not like a paella with artichokes.*
No nos gustan las novelas largas.	*We do not like long novels.*

Use the singular form if one or more infinitives follow **gustar**.

¿Te **gusta ir** al museo y **comprar** regalos allí?	*Do you like to go to the museum and buy gifts there?*
No nos **gusta lavar y planchar**.	*We do not like to wash and iron.*

The preposition **a**, followed by a pronoun or noun, is commonly used with **gustar** to clarify who is, or is not, pleased. The indirect noun or pronoun usually precedes the object pronoun.

A Juanita le gusta la pintura barroca.	*Juanita likes Baroque paintings.*
A él le gustan los cuadros de Dalí.	*He likes Dalí's paintings.*
Le gusta al guardia ese cuadro.	*The custodian likes this painting.*

Verbs like gustar

Many verbs follow the same pattern as **gustar**—that is, they are used with an indirect object pronoun.

VOCABULARIO			
aburrir	*to bore*	**fascinar**	*to fascinate, to love*
agradar	*to please*	**hacer falta**	*to miss, to need*
angustiar	*to worry*	**importar**	*to matter, to care about*
apasionar	*to excite, to thrill*	**interesar**	*to be interesting, appealing*
bastar	*to be enough*	**molestar**	*to annoy, to bother*
disgustar	*to upset*	**preocupar**	*to worry*
doler	*to hurt, to ache*	**quedar**	*to fit, to remain*
encantar	*to like thoroughly, to love*	**sobrar**	*to be left over*
faltar	*to lack, to be missing*	**tocar**	*to be one's turn*

Me aburre esta sinfonía.	*This symphony bores me.*
A Uds. les faltan diez euros.	*You are missing ten euros.*
Nos basta este dinero.	*This money is enough for us.*
¿Cómo **le queda a Ud.** la chaqueta?	*How does the jacket fit you?*

EJERCICIO 6·1

¡Practica! *Complete each sentence with the appropriate form of the pronoun and the present tense of the verb in parentheses.*

Modelo: No _____ coser y bordar (*to embroider*) todos los días.
(yo, gustar)

No *me gusta* coser y bordar todos los días.

1. A Mariana _____ mis palos de golf que son excelentes. (gustar)

2. _____ las Olimpiadas. (fascinar, él)

3. Este programa de yoga _____ mucho. (interesar, nosotras)

4. A vosotras _____ la conga y la salsa, bailes típicos del Caribe. (encantar)

5. _____ caminar por el parque todas las mañanas. (agradar, Uds.)

6. ¿_____ la actitud de Ada? Es muy competitiva. (disgustar, tú)

7. No _____ los mosquitos. Usamos el repelente para insectos. (molestar, nosotros)

8. Yo sé que a Uds. _____ las carreras de autos. (apasionar)

¡Practica! *Complete each sentence with the appropriate present tense form of the verb in parentheses.*

1. Me _____ los pies. Voy a comprar esos zapatos para caminar. (doler)

2. ¿Te _____ el precio de estas camisas? Yo tengo doscientos dólares en mi bolsillo. (preocupar)

3. A nosotros nos _____ solamente dos horas para elegir (*to choose*) los trajes. (quedar)

4. A Mara le _____ el dinero para comprar los esquís y los guantes. (sobrar)

5. Ahora les _____ a Uds. el turno y pueden pagar la tabla hawaiana. (tocar)

6. Sí, pero nos _____ también los bañadores, la sombrilla y el bronceador. (hacer falta)

7. ¿Les _____ a Uds. la opinión de la dependiente de la tienda? (importar)

8. A ellos les _____ cincuenta dólares para comprar los patines de ruedas (*roller skates*). (bastar)

Verbos como *gustar*. *Read the paragraph below, then underline the verb and the indirect object preceding it.*

Modelo: A ellos les cae mal el entrenador del gimnasio.

A ellos les cae mal el entrenador del gimnasio.

A toda la familia Sedano le encantan los deportes y las actividades al aire libre. Pedro Sedano tiene dos hijos. A Pablo, el mayor, le fascina esquiar y patinar sobre hielo. El más joven es Miguel y no le importa si hace frío o calor para jugar fuera de la casa. A Julia, la esposa de Sedano, le aburre quedarse en casa y le molestan los días cuando no hace ejercicio. A ella le bastan cien dólares al año para la suscripción del gimnasio. Ahora le quedan diez días para pagar la suscripción. Hoy le duele la cabeza. A esta familia no le hace falta una excusa para acampar o jugar fútbol en el parque. Se quedan en un hotel cerca de un lago.

Read the paragraph in Ejercicio 6-3 again and answer the questions below in complete sentences.

1. ¿Qué actividades le gustan a la familia Sedano?

_____

2. Y a Pablo, ¿qué le fascina?

_____

3. ¿Le importa a Miguel si hace frío o calor?

_____

4. ¿Qué le aburre a Julia?

_____

5. ¿Qué le duele hoy a Julia?

_____

Prepositions and prepositional phrases

VOCABULARIO

The following prepositions and prepositional phrases are commonly used in Spanish. You may use some of these in the exercises that follow.

a	*at, to*	**de**	*of*	**hacia**	*toward*
acerca de	*about*	**delante de**	*in front of*	**hasta**	*to, until, through*
fuera de	*outside of*	**dentro de**	*inside, within*	**para**	*for, to*
alrededor de	*around*	**desde**	*from, since*	**por**	*by, for, through*
ante	*before*	**detrás de**	*behind*	**según**	*according to*
con	*with*	**durante**	*during*	**sobre**	*above, over*
contra	*against*	**en**	*in*	**sin**	*without*

The prepositions **a** and **de** may be combined with other prepositions to form phrases such as **a favor de** (*in favor of*) and **en contra de** (*against*).

Tenemos dos votos **a favor de** Juan.   *We have two votes in favor of Juan.*
Estamos **en contra del** árbitro.   *We are against the referee.*

The prepositions **a** and **de** contract when they are followed by the masculine article **el**.

a + el → al; de + el → del.
¿Vamos **al** museo o no?   *Do we go to the museum or not?*
Regresamos **del** parque.   *We come back from the park.*

EJERCICIO
6·5

Preposiciones y frases. *Use one of the following prepositions to complete the sentences below.*

alrededor de	con	delante de	desde
durante	hasta	para	según

1. Ayer _____ toda la noche escuchamos a nuestros vecinos cantando en voz alta.

2. No terminaron _____ que llamamos a la puerta de su casa.

3. Todos estaban _____ un piano cuando llegamos allí.

4. Yo, _____ palabras claras, les dije que me encanta la música pero no a esa hora.

5. Entonces, nos invitaron a entrar a su casa _____ hablar con ellos.

6. Tienen ese piano en la sala _____ una ventana.

7. Y _____ ese momento, empezaron a tocar el piano y cantamos con ellos.

8. _____ la opinión de otros vecinos de nuestro barrio, esta familia no es antipática.

EJERCICIO
6·6

Y en tu caso, ¿verdadero (V) o falso (F)?

1. _____ Estoy a favor de la democracia.

2. _____ Estudio español en la computadora.

3. _____ No me levanto hasta el mediodía.

4. _____ Estoy en contra del reciclaje.

5. _____ En mi opinión, el karate es excelente.

6. _____ No sé nada sobre el fútbol americano.

Negative and affirmative words and expressions

In this chapter you have read examples with negative and affirmative words. Negative words and expressions state that something is not true. Affirmative words and expressions, on the contrary, assert or confirm ideas, statements, etc. Here are some commonly used negatives and their opposite affirmatives.

NEGATIVES		AFFIRMATIVES	
nada	*nothing*	**algo**	*something*
nadie	*no one, nobody, not anyone*	**alguien**	*someone, somebody, anyone*
ninguno, -a	*no, none, not anyone*	**alguno, -a**	*some, any*
ni... ni	*neither . . . nor*	**o... o**	*either . . . or*
no	*no, not*	**sí**	*yes*
nunca, jamás	*never, not ever*	**siempre**	*always*
sin	*without*	**con**	*with*
tampoco	*neither, not either*	**también**	*also*

- **Alguno, -a, algún** and **ninguno, -a, ningún** may function as adjectives.

Algunos estudiantes comen aquí.	*Some students eat here.*
Algunas mujeres usan estas chaquetas horribles.	*Some women wear these horrible jackets.*
Ningún enemigo va a ganar el trofeo.	*No enemy is going to win the trophy.*

- **Algo, alguien** and **nada, nadie** may function as indefinite pronouns.

Algo sucede aquí.	*Something is happening here.*
Alguien creativo diseña los zapatos.	*Someone creative designs the shoes.*
Nadie tiene una buena solución.	*No one has a good solution.*
¡**Nada** me importa!	*I do not care about anything!*

- **No** is the most common negative word used in Spanish. It precedes either the conjugated form of a verb or any object pronoun that precedes the verb.

No dices la verdad.	*You are not telling the truth.*
No me importa tu opinión.	*I do not care about your opinion.*

- In Spanish you may use double negatives that are unacceptable in English.

Elsa **no** dice **nunca** su fecha de nacimiento.	*Elsa never tells her date of birth.*
No sabe Ud. **nada** de matemáticas.	*You know nothing about math.*

- If a negative or an affirmative refers to a direct object pronoun, the personal preposition **a** must be placed *before* the negative or affirmative word.

No conozco **a nadie** como tú.	*I do not know anyone like you.*
¿Ves **a alguien** allí?	*Do you see anyone there?*

- **Ningún** and **algún** (shortened forms of **ninguno** and **alguno**) are used before a masculine singular noun and any feminine nouns that begin with a stressed **a-** or **ha-**.

No siento **ningún** dolor.	*I do not feel any pain.*
Algún día voy a visitar Brasil.	*Some day I will visit Brazil.*
Debe haber aquí **algún hacha**.	*There must be a hatchet here.*

Oposición. *Rewrite each sentence using the negative to contradict the underlined words.*

Modelo: Siempre cierro la puerta de mi casa.

   Nunca cierro la puerta de mi casa.

1. ¡Siempre necesitas mi ayuda!

   _____

2. ¿Ha venido alguna persona a tu casa?

   _____

3. Conozco a alguien como tú.

   _____

4. También conozco algunas de tus costumbres.

   _____

5. Conocemos a algunos de tus primos.

   _____

6. Tus amigos o te visitan o te saludan.

   _____

7. Necesitas algo, creo yo.

   _____

8. También sabes que soy muy cortés.

   _____

9. Sí, te puedo ayudar ahora.

   _____

Los pasatiempos y la diversión. Traducción. *Use the words in the* **Vocabulario útil** *for your translation.*

VOCABULARIO ÚTIL

billiards	**el billar**	*to bet*	**apostar (o → ue)**
board game	**el juego de mesa**	*to wait on line*	**hacer cola**
contestant	**el/la concursante**	*video game*	**el videojuego**
free time	**el tiempo libre**	*"Wheel of Fortune"*	**La ruleta de la suerte**
leisure	**el ocio**		

Sometimes I think that I like free time. But when I read the *Leisure* section in a newspaper, I do not know what to do. We have many options. No one likes to wait in line to buy tickets for a new film. I buy them online while I play a video game on my computer. I never play either board games or billiards. I watch "Wheel of Fortune." Some contestants bet and win a lot of money. I love to watch TV programs!

_____

_____

_____

_____

_____

_____

_____

_____

_____

Reflexive verbs and reflexive pronouns

You have probably learned about the reflexive and reflexive pronouns in Spanish because they are used frequently in daily routines. As learners and speakers of a language become fluent, they increasingly rely on pronouns.

The subject of a reflexive verb both performs and receives the action.

Me seco el pelo con la secadora.	*I dry my hair with a hairdryer.*

In this example, the reflexive pronoun **me** precedes the verb **seco**.
A negative word precedes the reflexive pronoun in Spanish.

No me levanto tarde.	*I do not get up late.*

If there is an infinitive verb or a present participle, the reflexive pronoun may either be placed before the conjugated verb or be attached to the infinitive.

Se quiere afeitar. / Quiere **afeitarse**.	*He wants to shave.*

A written accent is placed on the stressed vowel of the present participle when the reflexive pronoun is attached to it.

Se está **despertando**. / Está **despertándose**.	*She is waking up.*
Estamos **vistiéndonos**.	*We are getting dressed.*
Ella está **levantándose**.	*She is getting up.*

Reflexive pronouns

The reflexive pronouns are as follows.

SUBJECT PRONOUN	REFLEXIVE PRONOUN	SUBJECT PRONOUN	REFLEXIVE PRONOUN
yo	**me**	nosotros, -as	**nos**
tú	**te**	vosotros, -as	**os**
Ud.	**se**	Uds.	**se**
él/ella	**se**	ellos/ellas	**se**

In English, reflexive pronouns end in *-self* or *-selves* (*myself, ourselves*) and are the object of the verb.

Me miro en el espejo.   *I see **myself** in the mirror.*

In a nonreflexive construction, the subject is placed first followed by the verb (in this example the ending **-o** indicates the subject is **yo**).

Seco las toallas en la terraza.   *I dry the towels on the terrace.*

VOCABULARIO

Reflexive verbs are used to express or describe personal care and routines. This list includes reflexive verbs in the infinitive with the attached reflexive pronoun **se**. Verbs may have stem changes; some are irregular.

acostarse (o → ue)	*to go to bed*	**levantarse**	*to get up, stand up*
afeitarse	*to shave oneself*	**maquillarse**	*to put on makeup*
arreglarse	*to dress up*	**peinarse**	*to comb one's hair*
bañarse	*to bathe oneself*	**ponerse**	*to put on*
cepillarse	*to brush one's hair/teeth*	**quitarse**	*to take off*
despertarse (e → ie)	*to wake up*	**secarse**	*to dry oneself*
desvestirse (e → i)	*to undress oneself*	**verse**	*to see oneself*
dormirse (o → ue)	*to fall asleep*	**vestirse (e → i)**	*to dress oneself*
ducharse	*to take a shower*		
lavarse	*to wash oneself*		

Alina **se cepilla** los dientes.   *Alina brushes her teeth.*
Marian **se viste** rápido.   *Marian dresses quickly.*

In English, personal items are used with possessive pronouns; in Spanish, with its reflexive construction, the definite article is used.

Me quito el pijama y **me pongo** el vestido.   *I take off my pajamas and put on my dress.*

EJERCICIO
7·1

¡Práctica! *Complete each sentence with the appropriate reflexive pronoun and the present tense form of the verb in parentheses.*

1. Laura _____. (levantarse)

2. Sara entra al baño y _____. (ducharse)

3. Lorena y Cati _____ los dientes después de desayunar. (cepillarse)

4. Carmen y yo _____ todos los días. (maquillarse)

5. Juanito y tú _____ antes de bañarse. (desvestirse)

6. Y Uds., ¿_____ el pelo todas la mañanas? (secarse)

Traducción.

1. I go to bed early every night.

_____

2. Before I go to bed I get undressed.

_____

3. Then I put on my pajamas.

_____

4. I fall asleep around (**a eso de**) ten o'clock at night.

_____

5. At six o'clock in the morning I wake up.

_____

6. But I get up from bed half an hour later.

_____

7. Then I take a cold shower.

_____

8. I dry my hair.

_____

9. I do not shave.

_____

10. I brush my teeth in the morning at home.

_____

11. I put on a bit of makeup.

_____

12. I look at myself in the mirror.

_____

13. I get dressed before eight from Monday to Friday.

_____

14. Finally, I wash my hands and I am ready.

_____

Preguntas personales. *Answer the following questions in complete sentences.*

1. ¿Te levantas a la misma hora los fines de semana? ¿Por qué?

_____

2. ¿Te disgusta despertarte temprano los lunes? Explica.

_____

3. ¿Prefieres ducharte o bañarte?

_____

4. ¿Cómo te vistes cuando vas al trabajo?

_____

5. ¿Te tiñes (*to dye hair*) el pelo tú mismo?

_____

6. Yo me corto el pelo. ¿Y tú?

_____

In Spanish many verbs can be used as either reflexive or nonreflexive, for a subtle change in meaning. Some are irregular or have stem changes in the indicative present tense.

VOCABULARIO

Nonreflexive		Reflexive	
aburrir	*to bore someone*	aburrirse	*to become bored*
caer	*to fall*	caerse	*to fall down*
enojar	*to bother*	enojarse	*to get angry*
despertar (e → ie)	*to wake someone up*	despertarse (e → ie)	*to wake up*
dormir (o → ue)	*to sleep*	dormirse (o → ue)	*to fall asleep*
ir	*to go*	irse	*to go away*
llevar	*to carry*	llevarse	*to get along*
parecer	*to seem*	parecerse	*to resemble*
poner	*to place, put*	ponerse	*to put on; to become*
quitar	*to take away*	quitarse	*to take off*

Reflexive verbs may be used in all tenses, both simple and compound.

Lisa **se despertó** a la medianoche. *Lisa woke up at midnight.*

Juan Carlos **se levantaba** temprano *Juan Carlos used to wake up early*
todos los sábados. *every Saturday.*

The reflexive pronoun is usually placed before the auxiliary verb in compound tenses (see Chapter 17 for the perfect and the past perfect tenses).

Carlos **se ha escondido** detrás de *Carlos has hidden (himself) behind*
un árbol. *a tree.*

Pablito **se había caído** de la cama. *Pablito had fallen from his bed.*

EJERCICIO
7·4

¡Práctica! *Complete each sentence with the appropriate present tense form of the verb in parentheses.*

1. Beni _____ cuando está solo. (aburrirse)

2. Él y sus hermanos _____ mucho. (parecerse)

3. Hoy, Beni _____ a la casa de sus abuelos. (ir)

4. Antonia y Luis, los abuelos, no _____ cuando Beni va a su casa. (dormir)

5. A ellos les _____ que Beni es un fanático de la música del Caribe. (parecer)

6. Antonia _____ un canal hispano en la televisión y escuchan corridos mexicanos. (poner)

7. Luis _____ mientras Beni y Antonia hablan y escuchan el programa. (dormir)

8. Pero _____ furioso cuando lo despiertan para cantar con ellos. (ponerse)

9. Hoy _____ a visitarlos. (ir)

10. Beni _____ una guitarra para cantar con ellos. (llevar)

Traducción.

1. Your comments bore me.

_____

2. I am bored when I am alone.

_____

3. I am going to sleep now.

_____

4. You are bothering my dog.

_____

5. Money does not fall from the sky.

_____

6. My friend Alex wakes his children.

_____

7. I am going to take my mother to the dentist.

_____

8. I usually do not wake up late on weekends.

_____

9. I get angry if I do not sleep well.

_____

10. I take off my shoes and put on my slippers.

_____

11. I get along very well with my boss.

_____

12. When are you (*sing., fam.*) going away?

_____

13. I think you are going to visit Mila.

_____

14. I put my towels in the bathroom.

_____

15. I take my dogs to the park every day.

_____

Reflexive verbs and prepositions

As you have already seen, some verbs that are used in the reflexive form in Spanish are not usually reflexive in English. Many of these verbs are followed by a specific preposition.

VOCABULARIO

acordarse de	to remember	**morirse de**	to die of
atreverse a	to dare	**negarse a**	to refuse to
arrepentirse de	to regret	**olvidarse de**	to forget about
darse cuenta de	to realize	**parecerse a**	to resemble
burlarse de	to make fun of	**quejarse de**	to complain about
enterarse de	to find out about	**reírse de**	to make fun of
fijarse en	to take notice	**sorprenderse de**	to be surprised

---

Me quejo de mi jefe.	*I complain about my boss.*
¿Te burlas de mí?	*Are you making fun of me?*
Nos negamos a pagar la multa.	*We refuse to pay the fine.*
Uds. se olvidan de devolver los libros.	*You forget to return the books.*

EJERCICIO
7·6

¡Práctica! *Complete each sentence with the appropriate present tense form of the verb in parentheses.*

1. Jorge _____ y _____ de sus amigos. (burlarse, reírse)

2. Él no _____ de sus errores. (darse cuenta)

3. Nosotras _____ a limpiar este cuarto. (negarse)

4. Elli _____ de su jefe. (quejarse)

5. Uds. _____ a jugar este juego peligroso. (atreverse)

6. Marcos y yo siempre _____ de tu apellido. (olvidarse)

7. Siempre _____ de tus ideas fabulosas. (sorprenderse, yo)

EJERCICIO
7·7

Traducción.

1. Do you remember my friend Carlos?

_____

2. I make fun of my sister's boyfriend!

_____

3. I do not regret my comments.

_____

4. Now we find out about your lies.

_____

5. I do not complain about your questions.

_____

6. I am surprised because you are here!

_____

7. I realize that my car is not in the garage.

_____

8. I am dying of thirst!

_____

9. I do not dare to play golf with your father.

_____

10. I forget about everything!

_____

11. We refuse (**negarse**) to move to another city.

_____

Los buenos y los malos hábitos. Traducción. *Use the words in the* **Vocabulario útil** *for your translation.*

VOCABULARIO ÚTIL

according to	**de acuerdo a**	*lazy*	**haragán, -a; vago, -a**
nutritionist	**el/la nutricionista**	*past*	**el pasado**
need	**la necesidad**	*future*	**el futuro**

According to my nutritionist, we need to write two lists.

A list of good habits: to go to bed early and sleep eight hours, to get up early and to give thanks for a new day, to dare to change our daily routine, to forget about the past and think about the future, to find out about our friends' needs, to refuse to be lazy, and to remember life is short.

Reflexive verbs and reflexive pronouns **69**

And a short list of bad habits: to complain about everything, not to realize our good fortune, to make fun of other people's habits, and to forget tomorrow is another day.

_____

_____

_____

_____

_____

_____

_____

_____

Direct and indirect object pronouns and commands

·8·

In order to communicate more clearly and to avoid redundancy, we use pronouns—words that take the place of nouns. In this chapter you will review direct and indirect object pronouns. Remember that direct object pronouns receive the action of a verb, whereas indirect object pronouns point *to whom* or *for whom* the action is done.

Direct and indirect object pronouns

Let's review the direct and indirect object pronouns.

DIRECT OBJECT PRONOUN		INDIRECT OBJECT PRONOUN	
me	*me*	**me**	*to/for me*
te	*you* (fam.)	**te**	*to/for you* (fam.)
lo *you* (form.)	**los** *you* (form.)	**le** *to/for you* (form.)	**les** *to/for you* (form.)
lo *him*, **la** *her*	**los**, **las** *them*	**le** *to/for him/ her*	**les** *to/for them*

- ◆ Both direct and indirect object pronouns precede the conjugated verb.

Alicia ayuda **a Luis**. **Lo** ayuda.	*Alicia helps Luis. Alicia helps him.*
Ada trae el café **para Ana**. Ada **le** trae el café.	*Ada brings the coffee to Ana. Ada brings her coffee.*
No tienen **dinero**. No **lo** tienen.	*They don't have money. They don't have it.*
No doy regalos **a los chicos**. No **les** doy regalos.	*I don't give presents to the kids. I don't give them presents.*

- ◆ Direct and indirect object pronouns used with an infinitive or a present participle may either be attached to or precede the conjugated verb.

Lo quieres revisar. / Quieres revisar**lo**.	*You want to review it.*
Te debo responder la pregunta. / Debo responder**te** la pregunta.	*I should reply to your question.*

71

In order to keep the original stress, an accent is required on the stressed vowel when object pronouns are attached to a present participle.

Los estamos viendo. / Estamos viéndolos. *We are watching them.*
Los estoy lavando. / Estoy lavándolos. *I am washing them.*

EJERCICIO
8·1

Pronombres. *First replace the underlined words with the appropriate direct object pronoun. Then rewrite the sentence using this direct object pronoun.*

Modelo: Manolo lee la biografía de Vargas Llosa.

la; Manolo la lee.

1. Rosa recita dos poemas.

_____

2. Manolita está componiendo sus canciones.

_____

3. Mari no lleva los cuadernos a María José.

_____

4. Almodóvar hace reír a los actores.

_____

5. Yo llevo el agua para Marcela.

_____

6. Martín no quiere conocer a María Elena.

_____

7. Gustavo toca el piano y la guitarra.

_____

8. ¿Vas a incluirnos a nosotras en la lista?

_____

EJERCICIO
8·2

Pronombres y verbos reflexivos. *First replace the underlined words with the appropriate indirect object pronoun. Then rewrite the sentence using the indirect object pronoun in the appropriate position.*

Modelo: Voy a prestar una guitarra a mis vecinos.

les; Voy a prestarles una guitarra. / Les voy a prestar una guitarra.

1. Ángel está comprando creyones <u>para los niños necesitados</u>.

_____

2. Ali está llevando regalos <u>a los ancianos</u>.

_____

3. Raquel va a distribuir la comida <u>a los pobres</u>.

_____

4. Lalo y María no van a cantar canciones mexicanas <u>para los adultos</u>.

_____

5. Lola nunca puede prestar atención (*pay attention*) <u>a su colega Mario</u>.

_____

6. Margarita no quiere recitar sus poemas <u>a la audiencia</u> en el ayuntamiento (*city hall*).

_____

Double object pronouns

It is important to review the order of pronouns when both direct and indirect object pronouns are used in the same sentence.

- ◆ The indirect object pronoun precedes the direct object pronoun

  subject + indirect object pronoun + direct object pronoun + verb
  Junior **me lo** regala.   *Junior gives it to me.*

- ◆ Change **le** and **les** to **se** when they are followed by **lo**, **la**, **los**, or **las**

Carmen **le** da (a Ud.) **la nota**.	*Carmen gives the note to you.*
Carmen **se** la da.	*Carmen gives it to you.*
Ramón **le** pinta **un retrato**.	*Ramón paints a portrait for him.*
Ramón **se lo** pinta.	*Ramón paints it for him.*

Prepositional pronouns

Pronouns that follow a preposition are formed as follows.

SINGULAR		PLURAL	
mí	*me*	**nosotros, -as**	*we*
ti	*you* (fam.)	**vosotros, -as**	*you* (fam.)
usted (Ud.)	*you* (form.)	**ustedes (Uds.)**	*you* (form.)
él	*him, it*	**ellos**	*they*
ella	*her, it*	**ellas**	*they*

El regalo es **de él** para Lidia.   *The gift is from him to Lidia.*

There is also the emphatic prepositional pronoun (*yourself, himself, herself, itself; yourselves, themselves*).

Joel está fuera **de sí**.   *Joel is beside himself.*

Prepositional pronouns are used to emphasize or clarify a message, especially when double object pronouns are used.

Le doy **los cupones** de descuentos a Bella.   *I give Bella the discount coupons.*
Se los doy **a ella**, no **a ti**.   *I give them to her, not to you.*

EJERCICIO
8·3

Dos pronombres en una oración. *First replace the underlined words with the appropriate direct and indirect object pronouns. Then rewrite the sentence using these pronouns in the appropriate position.*

Modelo: Pedro lleva los postres a la familia.

los, le; Pedro se los lleva.

1. Carmen compra dos almohadas a sus hijos.

   _____

2. Ella prepara platos mexicanos a sus amigos.

   _____

3. Pedrito da agua a su hermana.

   _____

4. Raúl plancha las camisas para nosotros.

   _____

5. Carmen y Raúl están dando a los niños sus regalos de cumpleaños.

   _____

6. Marta compra libros a sus amigos.

   _____

7. ¿Marcos envió dos tarjetas a Uds.?

   _____

8. Manuel trae malas noticias a mí.

   _____

9. Yo compro las medicinas a mi tía.

   _____

10. Martín está enviando estas cartas a sus empleados.

    _____

Commands

When you need to give an order, advice, or a strong suggestion, you give commands directly to another person (*you*, singular or plural) using the imperative mood. Let's review how commands are formed and how to use them.

Regular affirmative **tú** commands

You give the familiar **tú** command to your family members, friends, classmates, or colleagues.

To form the **tú** commands, use the third person singular (**él**, **ella**, **usted**) form of the present indicative (you may want to review the present tense in Chapter 1). Note that some commands may include exclamation marks for emphasis. In Spanish, an inverted exclamation mark is placed at the beginning of the command.

Compra.	*Buy.*
Vende.	*Sell.*
¡Pide!	*Ask!*

Regular negative **tú** commands

To form familiar **tú** commands in the negative, use the first person singular (**yo**) form of the present tense, and replace the -**o** ending with -**es** for -**ar** verbs, and -**as** for -**er** and -**ir** verbs.

- -**ar** verbs   **mirar**   **mir**-o   **mir** + **es**

    No mires a esa persona.   *Don't look at that person.*

- -**er** verbs   **beber**   **beb**-o   **beb** + **as**

    No bebas el agua.   *Don't drink the water.*

- -**ir** verbs   **escribir**   **escrib**-o   **escrib** + **as**

    ¡No escribas la carta!   *Don't write the letter!*

Some verbs have spelling changes in the stem. In the following, the final consonant of the stem must be changed in order to preserve pronunciation.

- **c → qu**

    marcar, marc-a   No mar**ques** el número incorrecto.   *Don't dial the incorrect number.*

- **z → c**

    empezar, empiez-a   No empie**ces** a trabajar tarde.   *Don't start to work late.*

- **g → gue**

    colgar, cuelg-a   No cuel**gues** el teléfono.   *Do not hang up the phone.*

¡Órdenes! *Write the affirmative and negative familiar* **tú** *commands for each verb.*

1. cambiar _____; no _____

2. pedir _____; no _____

3. viajar _____; no _____

4. volver _____; no _____

5. dormir _____; no _____

6. pensar _____; no _____

7. correr _____; no _____

8. sufrir _____; no _____

9. leer _____; no _____

10. vender _____ no _____

Traducción. *Write the appropriate affirmative or negative familiar* **tú** *command.*

1. Use the new computer.

_____

2. Do not erase my notes.

_____

3. Put the paper in the printer.

_____

4. Please don't answer the phone.

_____

5. Go to your office now!

_____

6. Put away (**guardar**) these papers, please.

_____

7. Do not use these old keys.

_____

Irregular tú commands

A few verbs have irregular commands in the familiar **tú** form.

		AFFIRMATIVE COMMAND	NEGATIVE COMMAND
decir	*to say, tell*	di	no digas
hacer	*to do, make*	haz	no hagas
ir	*to go*	ve	no vayas
poner	*to put, place*	pon	no pongas
salir	*to leave, go out*	sal	no salgas
ser	*to be*	sé	no seas
tener	*to have*	ten	no tengas
venir	*to come*	ven	no vengas

Traducción. *Use the appropriate informal* **tú** *command.*

1. Put the bag on the floor.

_____

2. Leave at eight thirty today.

_____

3. Be careful (**tener cuidado**) because it's raining.

_____

4. Come early to class.

_____

5. Be (**ser**) courteous.

_____

6. Go to the market and buy bread.

_____

7. Tell the truth now.

_____

8. Do your work carefully.

_____

Traducción. *Use the appropriate informal* **tú** *command.*

1. Do not put your bag on my seat.

   _____

2. Do not leave the papers on the floor.

   _____

3. Don't have problems with your friends.

   _____

4. Do not come late to the theater.

   _____

5. Don't be ridiculous!

   _____

6. Do not go to the beach now.

   _____

7. Don't tell lies!

   _____

8. Do not make inappropriate comments.

   _____

Regular affirmative and negative formal **usted** commands

Use the formal **usted** command for people whom you address with respect, especially those you do not know well.

Suba usted, por favor.	*Go up, please.*
Hablen ustedes al gerente.	*Please speak to the manager.*

The regular **usted** commands are the same in both affirmative and negative. To form the **usted** commands, take the first person singular **yo** form of the present tense and replace the **-o** ending with **-e** for **-ar** verbs, and **-a** for **-er** and **–ir** verbs.

- ◆ -ar verbs   **bailar**   **bail-o**   **bail + e**

  Baile en la terraza.   **No baile** en la terraza.

  Dance on the terrace.   *Don't dance on the terrace.*

- ◆ -er verbs   **comer**   **com-o**   **com + a**

  ¡**Coma** chocolate!   ¡**No coma** chocolate!

  Eat chocolate!   *Don't eat chocolate!*

◆ -ir verbs   **abrir**   **abr**-o   **abr + a**

        Abra la carta.   **No abra la carta.**

        Open the letter.   *Don't open the letter.*

◆ Irregular **usted** commands

Only three verbs have irregular formal **usted** commands.

INFINITIVE	**USTED** COMMAND
saber	**sepa**
ser	**sea**
ir	**vaya**

EJERCICIO
8·8

En la oficina. *Write the appropriate affirmative and negative formal* **usted** *commands for each verb.*

1. (leer) las noticias   _____ ; _____

2. (contestar) las llamadas   _____ ; _____

3. (usar) las instrucciones   _____ ; _____

4. (recibir) a los clientes   _____ ; _____

5. (asistir) a la reunión esta mañana _____ ; _____

6. (ir) al aeropuerto   _____ ; _____

7. (ser) amable   _____ ; _____

8. (descansar) durante el almuerzo _____ ; _____

Regular affirmative and negative formal **ustedes** commands

To form the plural formal **ustedes** commands, simply add an **-n** to the singular formal **usted** command.

Viajen a las montañas.	*Travel to the mountains.*
No traigan los cupones vencidos.	*Do not bring the expired coupons.*
Salgan ya. **No vayan** muy tarde.	*Leave now. Do not go too late.*

Remember that the plural **ustedes** is used for both formal and familiar commands in most of the Hispanic world. The subject pronouns **usted** or **ustedes** sometimes may follow the verb as a sign of politeness.

Sí, por favor, **entre Ud.**	*Yes, please, come in.*
No **salgan Uds.** ahora.	*Do not leave now.*

Traducción. *Use the appropriate affirmative formal* **ustedes** *command.*

1. Turn to the right.

   _____

2. Follow the directions.

   _____

3. Find exit 45 on the turnpike (**autopista de peaje**).

   _____

4. Drive two miles after the exit.

   _____

5. Get to (**llegar**) Olmedo Street, number 114.

   _____

6. Park in front of our apartment building.

   _____

7. Ring the bell at the building entrance.

   _____

Affirmative and negative familiar **vosotros** commands

The familiar **vosotros** form is used only in peninsular Spanish. For affirmative commands of regular verbs, replace the final **-r** of the infinitive with **-d**. The only exception is with reflexive verbs: replace the final **-r** of the infinitive with the reflexive pronoun.

NONREFLEXIVE VERBS		REFLEXIVE VERBS	
Levantad el sofá.	*Lift the sofa.*	**Levantaos**.	*Stand up.*
Poned la ropa allí.	*Put the clothes there.*	**Poneos** la ropa.	*Put on your clothes.*
Vestid las muñecas.	*Dress the dolls.*	**Vestíos** ahora.	*Get dressed now.*

Negative **vosotros** commands for regular verbs are formed as follows.

-ar verbs:	**contar**	**cont-**	**cont + éis**	**No contéis** el dinero.
				Don't count the money.
-er verbs:	**temer**	**tem-**	**tem- + áis**	**No temáis.**
				Don't be afraid.
-ir verbs:	**ecribir**	**escrib-**	**escrib + áis**	¡**No escribáis** la carta!
				Don't write the letter!

Again, only three verbs have an irregular form of the negative **vosotros** commands.

saber	**No sepáis** las contraseñas.	*Do not know the passwords.*
ser	**¡No seáis** tacaños!	*Do not be stingy!*
ir	**No vayáis** por esa calle.	*Do not go down that street.*

Stem-changing **-ir** verbs again change **e** to **i** and **o** to u.

competir	**No compitáis.**	*Do not compete.*
dormir	**No durmáis.**	*Do not sleep.*
medir	**No midáis.**	*Do not measure.*
morirse	**No os muráis.**	*Do not die.*

EJERCICIO
8·10

En España. *Write the affirmative and negative* **vosotros** *commands for the following verbs.*

1. leer _____; no _____

2. dormir _____; no _____

3. sufrir _____; no _____

4. pensar _____; no _____

5. viajar _____; no _____

6. vivir _____; no _____

7. leer _____; no _____

8. caminar _____; no _____

9. conseguir _____; no _____

10. hacer _____; no _____

Pronouns with commands

Where do we place pronouns with commands?

- The direct and indirect object pronouns are always attached to the affirmative commands.

Cierra la puerta. Ciérra**la**.	*Close the door. Close it.*
Abra la clase para Miguel.	*Open the classroom for Miguel.*
Ábra**le** la clase.	*Open it for him.*

- The direct and indirect object pronouns are placed immediately before the verb in negative commands.

No cierres la puerta. No **la cierres**.	*Don't close the door. Do not close it.*
No abras el banco para Miguel.	*Do not open the bank for Miguel.*
No **lo abras**.	*Do not open it.*

To use the double object pronouns, follow the structure for affirmative and negative commands.

- affirmative command + indirect object pronoun + direct object pronoun

Regálame tu blusa. ¡Regál**amela**!   *Give me your blouse, give it to me!*

Devuelvan el regalo a José.   *Return the gift to José. Return it to him.*
Devuélvanselo.

- negative word + indirect object pronoun + direct object pronoun + negative command

No **me** digas **una mentira**.   *Don't tell me a lie.*
No **me la digas**.   *Do not tell it to me.*

EJERCICIO
8·11

¡Órdenes son órdenes! *Replace the underlined words with the appropriate direct and indirect object pronouns. Then rewrite the sentence using the direct and indirect object pronouns in the appropriate position.*

Modelo: Responde <u>las preguntas</u> <u>a tus amigos</u>.

           las, les; Respóndeselas.

1. Lee <u>el poema</u> <u>a tus amigos</u>.

_____

2. Anita, escribe <u>la lista de los regalos</u> <u>a tu mamá</u>.

_____

3. Da <u>el dinero</u> <u>a tu amiga</u>.

_____

4. No compren <u>los vegetales</u> <u>para mí</u>.

_____

5. Digan <u>sus nombres</u> <u>a la secretaria</u>.

_____

6. Sra. Blanco, cuente Ud. <u>sus problemas</u> <u>a su familia</u>.

_____

7. Abran <u>la puerta</u> <u>a esos señores</u>.

_____

8. No envíen <u>la invitación</u> <u>a mis hermanos</u>.

_____

Demonstrative and possessive adjectives and pronouns

·9·

Formerly you learned about adjectives and how to use them in Spanish to describe qualities, appearances of a person or objects, and quantities. However, demonstrative and possessive adjectives and pronouns have different functions, as we'll now review.

Demonstrative adjectives

Demonstrative adjectives point to the position of specific persons or things to which a speaker is referring. They precede the noun, with which they must agree in gender and number. In Spanish there are three demonstrative adjectives: **este**, **ese**, and **aquel**, and all their forms.

- ◆ **este** points out people or objects that are close to the speaker

    Este ejercicio es fácil.   *This exercise is easy.*

- ◆ **ese** indicates people or objects that are closer to the listener than to the speaker

    Esa computadora está muy cara.   *That computer is very expensive.*

- ◆ **aquel** shows people or objects that are far from both speaker and listener

    Aquellos monitores cuestan poco.   *Those monitors do not cost a lot.*

These three demonstrative adjectives decline as follows.

MASCULINE	FEMININE		MASCULINE	FEMININE	
este	**esta**	*this*	**estos**	**estas**	*these*
ese	**esa**	*that*	**esos**	**esas**	*those*
aquel	**aquella**	*that* (over there)	**aquellos**	**aquellas**	*those* (over there)

¿Necesitas **estas instrucciones**?   *Do you need these instructions?*
Quiero viajar en **ese auto**.   *I want to travel in that car.*
Luis trabaja en **aquella tienda**.   *Luis works in that store over there.*

En ese parque precioso. *Complete the paragraph below with the appropriate form of the demonstrative adjectives in parentheses.*

1. _____ (Este) verano voy a 2. _____ (ese) parques tranquilos con mi perro Max. Max corre alrededor de 3. _____ (aquel) dos lagos con 4. _____ (ese) patitos pequeños. 5. _____ (Aquel) peces tienen colores brillantes. Con 6. _____ (este) telescopio grande observo las estrellas y 7. _____ (aquel) planetas Venus y Marte. Escucho 8. _____ (aquel) cotorras (*parrot*) que hablan mucho. 9. _____ ¡(Este) vistas son impresionantes. 10. ¡_____ ¡(Este) parques son maravillosos!

En la joyería. Traducción.

1. This jewelry store is empty.

_____

2. Oh, these diamond rings must cost a fortune!

_____

3. Those earrings (**el arete**) are not cheap.

_____

4. Use (*pl., fam.*) that elevator over there to go to the second floor.

_____

5. In that shop window (**el escaparate**) they have pearls and emeralds.

_____

6. Those gentlemen over there love watches from Switzerland.

_____

7. I am ready to buy that gold bracelet.

_____

Possessive adjectives

You have read and reviewed the uses of prepositions in Chapter 6. In Spanish, the preposition **de** is used to express ownership.

la casa **de Alfonsina**		*Alfonsina's house*
los juguetes **de Pepito**		*Pepito's toys*

We use possessive adjectives to express the same idea of possession or ownership. Remember that there are two types of possessive adjectives in Spanish, short forms and long forms rather than the single form in English. The short forms agree in number but not gender with the object possessed, except for the **nosotros/vosotros** forms. All the long forms of possessive adjectives agree in gender and number with the object that someone or something owns.

SHORT FORMS		LONG FORMS	
mi *my*	**mis** *my*	**mío,-a** *my*	**míos,-as** *my*
tu (fam.) *your*	**tus** *your*	**tuyo, -a** (fam.) *your*	**tuyos, -as** (fam.) *your*
su *your*	**sus** *your*	**suyo, -a** *yours*	**suyos, -as** *yours*
su *his, her, its*	**sus** *his, her, its*	**suyo, -a** *his, her, its*	**suyos, -as** *his, her, its*
nuestro, -a *our*	**nuestros, -as** *our*	**nuestro, -a** *our*	**nuestros, -as** *our*
vuestro, -a *your*	**vuestros, -as** *your*	**vuestro, -a** *your*	**vuestros, -as** *your*
su *your*	**sus** *your*	**suyo, -a** *your*	**suyos, -as** *your*
su *their*	**sus** *their*	**suyo, -a** *his, her, its*	**suyos, -as** *their*

Now, let's review the position of these two possessive forms.

- The short forms are placed before the noun.

mi calendario	*my calendar*
nuestras tradiciones	*our traditions*

- The long forms are placed after the noun; they are used to express *of yours, of theirs*, etc.

un tío **tuyo**	*an uncle of yours*
los colegas **míos**	*colleagues of mine*
¡Ay, Dios **mío**!	*Oh, my God!*

- **Su, sus, suyo, suya, suyos,** and **suyas** have several meanings. It may sound repetitive, but to clarify the meaning of these forms, use this structure: article + noun + **de** + subject pronoun (**el** + **auto** + **de** + **ella**).

un amigo **de ellos**	*their friend, a friend of theirs*
los parientes **suyos**	*your relatives, relatives of yours*

EJERCICIO 9·3

Traducción. *Write the appropriate short form of the possessive adjective.*

1. my car _____

2. your (*sing., fam.*) bicycle _____

3. his skates_____

4. her taxi _____

5. our motorcycle _____

6. their fences (**la cerca**) _____

7. your (*pl., fam.*) neighbors _____

8. your (*pl., fam.*) garden _____

9. my trees _____

10. our building _____

EJERCICIO
9·4

Un viaje. *Write the long form of the possessive adjective to replace the underlined words.*

1. Aquí está <u>mi mapa</u>. _____

2. ¿Este es <u>tu calendario</u>? _____

3. Juan busca <u>su boleto</u>. _____

4. Alicia no encuentra <u>su mochila</u> (*backpack*). _____

5. Esos son <u>nuestros asientos</u>. _____

6. Julio tiene aquí <u>sus maletas</u>. _____

7. <u>Nuestro auto</u> está en el aparcamiento.

8. Aquí tenéis <u>vuestros sombreros</u>. _____

Demonstrative pronouns

The use of pronouns allows efficient, concise communication. Demonstrative pronouns are used to point at something that has been previously mentioned: *this, that one, that one over there,* and *these, those, those ones over there.* They have the same forms as the demonstrative adjectives, and reflect the gender and number of the noun they replace. Written accents are used only if it's necessary to distinguish the meaning.

SINGULAR			PLURAL		
masculine	feminine		masculine	feminine	
este	**esta**	*this one*	**estos**	**estas**	*these ones*
ese	**esa**	*that one*	**esos**	**esas**	*those ones*
aquel	**aquella**	*that one over there*	**aquellos**	**aquellas**	*those ones (over there)*

Tengo dos camisas. ¿Prefieres **esta** o **esa**?	*I have two shirts. Do you prefer this one or that one?*
Estos zapatos son caros pero **aquellos** son más baratos.	*These shoes are expensive but those ones are cheaper.*

The three demonstrative pronouns, **esto**, **eso**, and **aquello**, point to situations, ideas, etc., that are not clear or specified.

¿Por qué tienes **esto**?   *Why do you have this?*

Eso es un verdadero misterio.   *That is a real mystery.*

Y aquello, ¿qué es?   *And what is that over there?*

¡Práctica! *Write in the appropriate form of the demonstrative pronoun in parentheses that would replace each noun.*

1. los caminos _____ (este)

2. las salidas _____ (aquel)

3. los pueblos _____ (ese)

4. las avenidas _____ (esta)

5. el almacén _____ (aquel)

6. la calle _____ (aquel)

7. la estación _____ (ese)

8. los autobuses _____ (este)

9. el chofer _____ (aquel)

10. las motos _____ (esta)

Traducción.

1. Why do you want this?

_____

2. This is my umbrella and that one is Manuel's umbrella.

_____

3. I have a raincoat but I like this one.

_____

4. Molly does not have a hat. She needs that one over there.

_____

5. And that over there, what is it?

_____

Possessive pronouns

The possessive pronouns have the same forms as the long forms of possessive adjectives. They agree in gender and number with the noun they replace. Note that the Spanish possessive pronoun is always preceded by the definite article **el**, **la**, **los**, or **las**.

	SINGULAR	PLURAL
mine	**el mío, la mía**	**los míos, las mías**
yours (*fam.*)	**el tuyo, la tuya**	**los tuyos, las tuyas**
yours	**el suyo, la suya**	**los suyos, las suyas**
his, hers, its	**el suyo, la suya**	**los suyos, las suyas**
ours	**el nuestro, la nuestra**	**los nuestros, las nuestras**
yours	**el vuestro, la vuestra**	**los vuestros, las vuestras**
theirs	**el suyo, la suya**	**los suyos, las suyas**

No tengo mi cámara. Necesito **la tuya**.   *I do not have my camera. I need yours.*

Nuestra tienda abre a las ocho pero   *Our store opens at eight but yours does not*
   la suya no abre hasta las nueve.   *open until nine.*

VOCABULARIO

Review this vocabulary before doing the exercises that follow.

la almohada	*pillow*	**el maquillaje**	*make-up*	**el peine**	*comb*
el despertador	*alarm clock*	**la navaja de afeitar**	*razor*	**la toalla**	*towel*
el espejo	*mirror*	**la pasta de dientes**	*toothpaste*	**la sábana**	*sheet*

EJERCICIO
9·7

¿De quién es? *Write in the appropriate form of the possessive pronoun.*

Modelo: ¿Ese peine? Es _____. (*mine*)

         Es *el mío*.

1. ¿Estas toallas? Son _____. (*ours*)

2. ¿Y esta pasta de dientes? ¿Es _____, Marisa? (*yours*)

3. ¿De quién son estas sábanas? Estas son _____, de Marta y mía. (*ours*)

4. ¿Y este despertador? Ah, es _____. (*yours*, **Ud.**)

5. ¿Este maquillaje? Creo que es _____. (*hers*)

6. ¿Estos espejos? ¿Estos son _____, Laurita y Sara? (*yours*, **vosotros**)

7. ¿Estas dos almohadas? Sí, son _____. (*theirs*)

8. ¿La navaja de afeitar? Pues, es _____. (*ours*)

Idiomatic verbal phrases

You probably remember and have used various common expressions that include Spanish verbs. Idiomatic verbal phrases help you to communicate more clearly in Spanish, but as with any idiom they can rarely be translated word for word. In this chapter, you will review many commonly used expressions with **dar**, **estar**, **hacer**, and **tener**.

Expressions with **dar**

These idiomatic constructions consist of a conjugated form of the verb **dar** followed immediately by a preposition or an article + noun.

Dar + preposition

In these idiomatic expressions the preposition may be followed by an infinitive. As you have already reviewed in Chapter 7, when **dar** is used reflexively the pronoun **se** is attached to the infinitive (**darse**).

dar a entender que	*to imply that*
dar a	*to face, look out on*
dar con	*to find, run into*
dar contra	*to hit, knock against*
dar cuerda a	*to wind (up)*
dar ganas de	*to feel like*
dar recuerdos a	*to give regards*
darse cuenta de	*to realize*
darse por vencido	*to give in, give up*
darse prisa	*to hurry*

Mis ventanas **dan al** patio.	*My windows face the back yard.*
Ayer **dimos con** unos amigos en una farmacia.	*Yesterday we ran into some friends at a pharmacy.*
El auto **dio contra** una cerca.	*The car hit a fence.*
Es tarde y me **dan ganas de** dormir.	*It's late and I feel like sleeping.*
Nos **dimos cuenta de** un error con las respuestas.	*We realized we made a mistake with one of the answers.*
Nunca **me doy por vencido**.	*I never give up.*
No **te des prisa**. Es temprano.	*Do not hurry. It is early.*

Dar + article and noun

dar la hora	*to strike the hour*
dar las gracias	*to thank*
dar un abrazo	*to hug, embrace*
dar un paseo	*to take a walk, ride*
dar un saludo a alguien	*to greet, say hello to someone*
dar una vuelta	*to take a walk, ride*
darse la mano	*to shake hands*

El reloj **dio las dos**.	*The clock struck two.*
Dimos un paseo con José por el parque.	*We took a walk with José through the park.*
Se saludaron y **se dieron la mano**.	*They said hello and shook hands.*
Dale saludos a tu hermano.	*Say hello to your brother.*

EJERCICIO
10·1

Expresiones en español. *Fill in the blank with the letter of the phrase in the second column that expresses a similar meaning to the sentence in the first column.*

1. _____ Tengo sueño.

2. _____ Caminamos por el parque.

3. _____ ¡Tiene que llegar a la oficina pronto!

4. _____ Encontramos la joyería al sur de esta calle.

5. _____ Recuerdos para tu padre de mi parte.

6. _____ ¡No puede ganar!

7. _____ Ahora sé que tenía un error en mi examen.

8. _____ La pelota rompió la ventana.

a. Dar un paseo

b. Dar con

c. Dar saludos

d. Dar ganas de dormir

e. Darse cuenta de

f. Darse prisa

g. Darse por vencido

h. Dar contra

Expressions with estar

In these idiomatic expressions, **estar** usually translates into English as *to be*. You may want to review the information in Chapter 3 on the different uses of **ser** and **estar**.

Estar + preposition + infinitive

estar al caer	*to be about to happen*
estar al corriente de	*to be up to date*
estar a punto de	*to be just about to*
estar para	*to be about to*

estar por	*to be inclined to*
Ahora **está a punto de llover**.	*It is just about to rain.*
Los padres **están al corriente de** los problemas de sus hijas.	*The parents are up-to-date with their daughters' problems.*
Estamos listos **para salir** a eso las diez.	*We are about to leave around ten o'clock.*
Estoy por perder la calma porque me interrumpen.	*I am about to lose my patience because they interrupt me.*

Estar + adjective or preposition

estar apurado/-a	*to be in a hurry*
estar conforme (con)	*to be in agreement (with), agree*
estar de acuerdo con	*to be in agreement with, agree*
estar de buen/mal humor	*to be in a good/bad mood*
estar de paso	*to be passing through*
estar de vuelta	*to come back, return*
estar fuera de sí	*to be beside oneself*
estar por	*to be in favor of*

Los viajeros **estaban** muy **apurados** para llegar a su destino.	*The travelers were in a hurry to get to their destination.*
Estamos de acuerdo con tu opinión.	*We agree with your opinion.*
¿Por qué **están ellos de mal humor**? Porque sus amigos **están de paso** para viajar.	*Why are they in a bad mood? Because their friends are passing through.*
Probablemente **estarán de vuelta** pronto.	*Probably they will be back soon.*
¡**Estoy fuera de mí**! No sé cómo arreglar mi auto.	*I am beside myself! I do not know how to fix my car.*
Estoy por el equipo de Argentina porque van a ganar.	*I am for the Argentina team because they are going to win.*

EJERCICIO
10·2

Traducción.

1. I am just about to finish my answers on this sheet of paper.

_____

2. I am inclined to go to out.

_____

3. I do not agree with your (**tú**) ideas.

_____

4. I am not in a good mood if I do not take a nap (**la siesta**) in the afternoon.

_____

5. I will be back here around midnight.

_____

6. I am not in a hurry. I can wait for a few minutes.

_____

Expressions with hacer

In Spanish there are many useful verbal expressions with the verb **hacer**.

Expressions with hacer to describe the weather

Note that these are impersonal expressions that use the third person singular.

hacer buen tiempo	*to be good weather*
hacer mal tiempo	*to be bad weather*
hacer calor/frío	*to be hot/cold*
hacer sol	*to be sunny*
hacer viento	*to be windy*
hacer fresco	*to be chilly*

Hace mucho calor ahora.	*It is too hot now.*
No **hace frío** aquí.	*It is not cold here.*
En Chicago **hace mucho viento**.	*It is very windy in Chicago.*

Other expressions with hacer

hacer caso (a)	*to pay attention*
hacer(se) daño	*to harm/hurt (oneself)*
hacer(le) daño a alguien	*to harm/hurt someone*
hacer el equipaje	*to pack a bag*
hacer una lista	*to make a list*
hacer la maleta	*to pack a bag*
hacer pregunta(s)	*to ask question(s)*
hacer un recado	*to run an errand*
hacer un viaje	*to take a trip*
hacer una visita	*to pay a visit*

Ali no le **hace caso** a su siquiatra.	*Ali doesn't pay attention to her psychiatrist.*
Hicimos las maletas ayer.	*We packed our bags yesterday.*
Hicimos un viaje a Quito el año pasado.	*We took a trip to Quito last year.*
Te haces daño con ese martillo.	*You are hurting yourself with that hammer.*

Mis planes. *Choose from expressions with* **hacer** *to complete each sentence.*

Modelo: Hoy aquí _____. La temperatura está a 70 grados.

Hoy aquí *hace fresco*. La temperatura está a 70 grados.

1. Mañana voy a _____ a Colorado.

2. Voy a _____ para mi esposa y comprar algo antes de viajar.

3. Ella quiere _____ a su hermana en San Diego para descansar unos días.

4. Mi esposa, Ana, nunca puede _____ a su doctora y no sigue sus recomendaciones.

5. Una persona puede _____ si no pone atención a su médico.

6. Yo voy a _____ de lo que debemos hacer: más ejercicio todos los días, más salud, etc.

7. Aquí en Sacramento puede _____ casi todo el año y no usamos el aire acondicionado.

8. Pues bien, no viajamos entonces. No hay que _____.

Y en tu caso, ¿verdadero (V) o falso (F)?

1. _____ No hago mis maletas cuando viajo.

2. _____ Hago muchas preguntas en español a mis amigos.

3. _____ Todos los años hago una visita a unos amigos en Canadá.

4. _____ Quiero hacer un viaje a Uruguay.

5. _____ Me gusta cuando hace calor.

6. _____ No hago caso a lo que dice mi horóscopo.

7. _____ Si hace mal tiempo, no salgo de casa.

8. _____ Estoy por terminar mi trabajo en casa ahora.

Expressions with tener

The English verb *to be* is used to translate many expressions with the verb **tener**. Let's review the meaning of these expressions in three groups.

Expressing physical sensations

tener calor	*to feel warm*
tener frío	*to be cold*
tener dolor de cabeza	*to have a headache*
tener dolor de estómago	*to have a stomachache*
tener dolor de muela	*to have a toothache*
tener hambre/sed	*to be hungry/thirsty*
tener sueño	*to be sleepy*
Ay, ¡**tengo un dolor de muela**!	*Oh, I have a toothache!*
¿**Tienes hambre?**	*Are you hungry?*
Tengo sueño y voy a dormir.	*I am sleepy and I am going to bed.*

As you know, not all feminine nouns end in -a—for instance, **la sed** and **el hambre** are feminine. In Spanish, nouns that start with the stressed **a-** or **ha-** are feminine, and they take the definite article **el: el águila negra, el hacha rota.**

Tengo mucha hambre.	*I am very hungry.*

Expressing psychological sensations

tener celos (de)	*to be jealous*
tener confianza en	*to be/feel confident in*
tener cuidado	*to be careful*
tener (la) culpa de	*to be guilty of*
tener miedo a/de	*to be afraid of*
tener (el) orgullo	*to be proud*
tener prisa	*to be in a hurry*
tener vergüenza de	*to be ashamed of*
Tengo celos. ¡Helena siempre gana!	*I am jealous. Helena always wins!*
Julio **tiene mucho cuidado** cuando viaja.	*Julio is very careful when he travels.*
No **tengas prisa.** Podrás hacerlo pronto.	*Don't be in a hurry. You will be able to do it soon.*
Tenemos miedo de perder el autobús.	*We are afraid we're going to miss the bus.*
No le **tengo miedo a** nadie.	*I am not afraid of anyone.*
Tengo el orgullo de presentar a Mía.	*I am proud to introduce Mía.*

Other expressions with **tener**

tener (la) suerte	*to be lucky*
tener... años	*to be . . . years old*
tener en cuenta	*to take into account*
tener éxito	*to be successful*
tener ganas de	*to feel like, want to*
tener lugar	*to take place, be at*

tener mala suerte	*to be unlucky*
tener que ver con	*to have to do with*
tener razón	*to be right*

¿**Tienes ganas de** bailar esta noche?	*Do you feel like dancing tonight?*
Ellos **tienen razón**.	*They are right.*
Tengo solamente **veinte años**.	*I am only twenty years old.*
El campeonato **tuvo lugar** en Londres.	*The championship took place in London.*
Tienes mala surte: no ganó tu equipo.	*You are unlucky: your team did not win.*
¿**Esto tiene que ver** con los problemas de tu familia?	*Does this have to do with your family's problems?*

EJERCICIO 10·5

Expresiones en español. *Fill in the blank with the letter of the phrase in the second column that has a similar meaning to the sentence in the first column.*

1. _____ Necesita una chaqueta y un suéter.   a. Tiene éxito.

2. _____ Trabaja en una compañía y es su presidenta.   b. Tiene mucha suerte.

3. _____ La casa está oscura y no quiere entrar.   c. Tiene razón.

4. _____ Gana dinero en la lotería.   d. Tiene calor.

5. _____ Necesita dos aspirinas.   e. Tiene prisa.

6. _____ Camina rápido para llegar a su oficina.   f. Tiene sueño.

7. _____ Sube a su dormitorio y se acuesta.   g. Tiene frío.

8. _____ No se equivoca.   h. Tiene miedo.

9. _____ Necesita el aire acondicionado.   i. Tiene dolor de cabeza.

10. _____ Comete varios errores y se siente mal.   j. Tiene vergüenza.

EJERCICIO 10·6

En la clínica. Traducción. *Use the appropriate **tú** form of the present tense. Use the words in the **Vocabulario útil** for your translation.*

VOCABULARIO ÚTIL

doctor, physician	**el médico / la médica**	*psychiatrist*	**el/la siquiatra**
health	**la salud**	*sane*	**cuerdo, -a**
needle	**la aguja**	*surgeon*	**el cirujano / la cirujana**
nurse	**el enfermero / la enfermera**		

1. Are you cold or warm?

   _____

2. You are afraid of the needle.

   _____

3. You do not have confidence in the surgeon.

   _____

4. You are not afraid of the dark.

   _____

5. The psychiatrist is right. You are sane.

   _____

6. You are in a hurry to leave the clinic.

   _____

7. Are you sleepy? I'll turn off the light.

   _____

8. You are lucky. This nurse is excellent.

   _____

9. You are forty years old and you are healthy.

   _____

10. Now you are hungry and you are ready to go home.

   _____

Interrogatives and exclamations

Interrogatives are the words used to request information, or to ask questions of other people. Exclamations are used to express different emotions.

Interrogative words

Interrogative words may function as adjectives, pronouns, or adverbs. Remember that in Spanish an inverted question mark must precede the interrogative sentence or phrase. Here are some frequently used interrogatives.

¿cuál? ¿cuáles?	*which?*
¿cuánto? ¿cuánta?	*how much?*
¿cuántos? ¿cuántas?	*how many?*
¿qué?	*what?*
¿quién? ¿quiénes?	*who?*
¿a quién? ¿a quiénes?	*whom?*

Interrogative adjectives

The interrogative adjective precedes a noun.

¿**Qué nota** tienes en la clase de español?	*What grade do you have in your Spanish class?*
¿**Cuánto dinero** ganas ahora?	*How much money do you earn now?*
¿**Cuántos autos** están en el parqueo?	*How many cars are in the parking lot?*

Interrogative pronouns

Interrogative pronouns are used to ask questions about something previously mentioned, and are followed by a verb.

Juan está aquí, con nosotros. ¿**Quién es** Juan?	*Juan is with us, here. Who is Juan?*
Hay **muchos camareros** en la cocina. ¿**Cuántos están** allí?	*There are many waiters in the kitchen. How many are there?*

Interrogative adverbs

¿cómo?	*how?*
¿cuándo?	*when?*
¿dónde?	*where?*
¿adónde?	*where to?*
¿para qué?	*why?* (purpose)
¿por qué?	*why?* (reason)

Interrogative adverbs are placed before the verb, unless there is an object pronoun or a negative word in the interrogative sentence.

¿Adónde va aquella señora?	*Where is that lady going?*
¿Cómo le va?	*How are you doing?*
¿Cuándo ves a Gabriela?	*When do you see Gabriela?*
¿Por qué no viene Gabi contigo?	*Why doesn't Gabi come with you?*
¿Para qué necesitas este libro?	*Why do you need this book?*

Also, we may ask ourselves questions when we are in doubt.

¿Dónde puse la llave de la casa?	*Where did I put the house key?*

Note the difference in the meanings and uses of **¿por qué?** and **¿para qué?** Both translate as *why?*

- **¿Por qué?** → **Porque** = *because* (reason)

¿Por qué no viene Zoe aquí?	*Why isn't Zoe coming here? Because*
Porque está cansada.	*she is tired.*

- **¿Para qué?** → **Para** = *for* (purpose)

¿Para qué trae Ud. esa maleta?	*Why do you bring that bag?*
Para devolverla a su hermana.	*In order to return it to your sister.*

**EJERCICIO
11·1**

Traducción.

1. What are you doing (*fam., sing.*) now?

   _____

2. Whom do you (*fam., sing.*) see here?

   _____

3. Who are your (*fam., sing.*) friends?

   _____

4. Which one of these tables do you want (*fam., sing.*)?

   _____

5. Which of these games do you play (*fam., sing.*), chess or dominoes?

   _____

6. How much money do you pay (*fam., sing.*) for these ridiculous shoes?

   _____

7. How much patience do you have (*fam., sing.*) with your friends?

   _____

8. How many books do you read (*fam., sing.*) every year?

   _____

9. How many girlfriends do you have (*fam., sing.*) in your neighborhood?

   _____

10. How can you read (*fam., sing.*) and listen at the same time?

    _____

11. When do you go (*fam., sing.*) to California?

    _____

12. Where is my money?

    _____

13. Where am I going tonight? I don't know.

    _____

14. Why don't I have a job? I am lazy.

    _____

15. Why do I use this book every day? It helps me to learn Spanish!

    _____

EJERCICIO
11·2

Una entrevista. *Supply an answer to each question in the* **Ud.** *form of the present tense.*

Modelo: (quien) *¿Quiénes son Uds.?*

            Ana Moncada y mi esposo, Juan Villalba.

1. ¿_____?

El senador Julián del Portal.

2. ¿_____?

Vivo en Carabobo, Venezuela.

3. ¿————————————————————————?

Tengo dos hijas.

4. ¿————————————————————————?

Se llaman Ali y Mari.

5. ¿————————————————————————?

Ali tiene dieciséis y Mari dieciocho.

6. ¿————————————————————————?

Viajo a Miami porque me gustan la ciudad y las playas.

7. ¿————————————————————————?

Regreso a Venezuela la semana próxima.

8. ¿————————————————————————?

¿Mi profesión? Soy dentista.

More about interrogative pronouns qué and cuál

The two interrogative pronouns **qué** (*what*) and **cuál** (*which*) are used for different purposes.

- As an interrogative, the pronoun **qué** asks for an explanation, definition, description, or general information. It precedes a verb or a noun.

¿**Qué** es un satélite artificial?	*What is an artificial satellite?*
¿**Qué** quieres ahora?	*What do you want now?*

- **Qué** used before a noun can function as an adjective.

¿**Qué hora** es?	*What is the time?*
¿**Qué campeonatos** ganaste?	*What championships did you win?*

- **Cuál** (pl. **cuáles**) is used to ask more specific questions and to distinguish one item among others. Note that no nouns follow **cuál** or **cuáles**.

Tengo dos. ¿**Cuál** quieres?	*I have two. Which (one) do you want?*
¿**Cuáles** necesitas, los platos o las tazas?	*Which (ones) do you need, the dishes or the cups?*

- **Qué**, **cuál**, and **cuáles** are used in indirect questions.

No entiendo **qué** debo hacer.	*I do not understand what I should do.*
Él puede adivinar **cuáles** van a ganar.	*He can predict which ones will win.*

Preguntas en español. *Choose the appropriate interrogative word for each question.*

adónde   cómo   cuál   cuáles   cuándo

cuánta   cuántas   cuántos   dónde   qué

1. ¿_____ vas los fines de semana?

2. ¿_____ vives, en una ciudad o en el campo?

3. ¿_____ celebras tu cumpleaños? ¿El cinco de agosto?

4. ¿_____ es esto? ¿Un regalo para ti?

5. ¿_____ hermanos tienes? ¿Muchos?

6. ¿_____ horas duermes cada día?

7. ¿_____ prefieres, los colores oscuros o los claros?

8. ¿_____ es tu deporte favorito?

9. ¿_____ son tus amigos? ¿Son chistosos y alegres?

10. ¿_____ paciencia tienes? ¿Poca o mucha?

¿Qué, cuál o cuáles? *Complete each sentence with the appropriate interrogative.*

1. ¿_____ es tu actividad favorita?

2. ¿_____ piensas acerca de los hobbies?

3. Entonces, ¿_____ es un hobby para ti, un entretenimiento o un oficio?

4. ¿_____ son los nombres de tus cantantes favoritos?

5. ¿Sabes _____ ingredientes necesitas para hacer tamales mexicanos?

6. ¿_____ son los mejores pasatiempos, los rompecabezas (*puzzle*) o los crucigramas?

7. Si quieres jugar con una tenista famosa, ¿_____ es su nombre?

8. ¿_____ opinas acerca del boxeo?

9. ¿_____ prefieres, actividades al aire libre o leer en un sillón cómodo?

Exclamations

Exclamation words are used to express emotions such as surprise, happiness, sadness, and so on. Note that in Spanish an inverted exclamation mark must precede an exclamation word, whether this is the first word of a sentence or of a phrase. Each exclamation word takes a written accent.

Frequently used exclamation words

The following words precede a noun, adjective, or adverb.

¡qué!	*what! how!*
¡cómo!	*how!*
¡cuánto! ¡cuánta!	*how (much)!*
¡cuántos! ¡cuántas!	*how (many)!*

¡Qué año hemos tenido!	*What a year we had!*
¡Qué difícil ha sido!	*How difficult it's been!*
¡Qué fácilmente se gasta el dinero!	*How easily we spend the money!*
¡Cuánto trabajo!	*So much work!*

En el aeropuerto. *Underline the appropriate exclamation word for each sentence.*

Modelo: ¡(Cuánto / <u>Qué</u>) rápido pasa el tiempo!

1. ¡Mira, (qué / cuánto) grande es el avión!

2. ¡Ay, (qué / cuánto) tiempo! ¡Dos horas más antes de salir del aeropuerto!

3. ¡(Cuánto / Cuántos) viajeros hay aquí!

4. Un día difícil. ¡(Qué / Cómo) día!

5. ¡Por Dios, (cuántos / cuántas) niños están durmiendo en el piso!

6. ¡(Cómo / Qué) rápido sube aquel avión!

7. ¡(Cómo / Qué) lento (*slowly*) pasa el tiempo cuando tenemos que esperar!

8. ¡(Cómo / Qué) mala suerte! No tengo un asiento todavía para viajar.

Traducción. *Review the words in the* **Vocabulario útil** *before doing the following exercise.*

VOCABULARIO ÚTIL

advisor	**el asesor / la asesora**	*portfolio*	**la cartera de inversiones**
economy	**la economía**	*to save*	**ahorrar**

Good luck!	¡Buena suerte!	stable	estable
happiness	la alegría, la felicidad	stock market	la bolsa de valores
to invest	invertir	stocks	las acciones (de valores)
madness	la locura		

1. What? Max wants to invest two thousand dollars in the stock market.

_____

2. Why not? Max does not want to save (ahorrar) money in the bank.

_____

3. He thinks he can make money in six months. Good luck!

_____

4. What madness! The economy is not stable now.

_____

5. What do I have in my portfolio?

_____

6. How many shares of excellent companies in the USA?

_____

7. What happiness! Today the stock market wins.

_____

8. But what is going to happen tomorrow? Who knows!

_____

9. How can we follow the economic situation in the whole world?

_____

10. Who is your advisor?

_____

Regular verbs in the preterit tense

Previously you have learned the preterit tense in Spanish and used it to describe actions that took place in the past. In this chapter you will review and learn more about the preterit and its uses.

The preterit tense

The preterit allows us to refer to and talk about actions and events that were completed in the past. These include actions or events that either happened or began in the past, actions that took place a specific number of times, or actions that were completed at a specific time.

Let's review some of the uses for the preterit and consider the examples included for each use.

- An action completed in the past

Salieron a pasear por el puente.	*They went out to walk on the bridge.*
Mari y yo **cenamos** en la terraza.	*Mari and I had dinner on the terrace.*
Empezó a caminar después de cenar.	*He started to walk after having dinner.*

- A series or sequence of actions completed in the past

Tronó, llovió y **escampó**.	*It thundered, it rained, and it stopped raining.*
Mirta **bostezó, se acostó** y **se quedó** dormida.	*Mirta yawned, went to bed, and fell asleep.*

In the following examples you will see actions that took place at a specific time, measured either by a calendar, seasons, or the clock, or the number of times the action happened.

- Actions that took place, began, or ended at a specific time

Salimos a las ocho de la noche.	*We left at eight o'clock at night.*
El partido **empezó** justo a las dos de la tarde.	*The game started at two o'clock in the afternoon.*
El verano pasado **viajamos** a Sicilia.	*Last summer we traveled to Sicily.*

- Actions that began or were completed in the past at a specific time

El concierto **empezó a tiempo**.	*The concert started on time.*
La tienda **cerró a las seis**.	*The store closed at six o' clock.*
No **trabajaron los lunes**.	*They did not work on Mondays.*

- Actions that occurred a specific number of times

| **Viajé** a Miami **tres veces** este verano. | *I traveled to Miami three times this summer.* |
| Mis amigos me **pidieron** ayuda durante **cinco días** para pintar su casa. | *My friends asked me for help during five days to paint their house.* |

As you have seen in these examples, the preterit indicates *when, at what time*, or *how many times* an action or actions took place in the past.

Formation of the preterit tense

Use these rules to conjugate the regular verbs in the preterit: drop the infinitive ending (-**ar**, -**er**, -**ir**) and add the following preterit endings:

-**ar** verbs: -**é**, -**aste**, -**ó**, -**amos**, -**asteis**, -**aron**

-**er** verbs: -**í**, -**iste**, -**ió**, -**imos**, -**isteis**, -**ieron**

-**ir** verbs: -**í**, -**iste**, -**ió**, -**imos**, -**isteis**, -**ieron**

The preterit tense for all conjugations is as follows.

caminar to *walk*	**vender** to *sell*	**abrir** to *open*
caminé	vendí	abrí
caminaste	vendiste	abriste
caminó	vendió	abrió
caminamos	vendimos	abrimos
caminasteis	vendisteis	abristeis
caminaron	vendieron	abrieron

The first and third person singular forms of regular verbs in all three conjugations require a written accent on the ending.

| **Salí** al patio y **limpié** las sillas. | *I went out to the patio and I cleaned the chairs.* |
| Julián **ayudó** a sus amigos ayer. | *Julián helped his friends yesterday.* |

Note that -**ar** and -**ir** verbs have the same form in the present and preterit tenses in the first person plural. The context of a sentence usually includes an adverb that indicates whether the tense used is the present or the preterit.

| **Ahora caminamos** por el parque. | *Now we are walking through the park.* |
| **Ayer abrimos** la tienda temprano. | *Yesterday we opened the store early.* |

¡Práctica! *Complete each sentence with the appropriate preterit tense form of the verb in parentheses.*

1. Anoche mi esposa Gabriela _____ de su oficina a las siete de la noche. (salir)

2. Yo _____ la puerta de nuestro apartamento. (abrir)

3. Después, ella y yo _____ la cena. (preparar)

4. Dos amigos _____ a la puerta para saludarnos. (llamar)

5. Desde la cocina, Gabi _____ a Samuel y a Tomás. (saludar)

6. A eso de (*About*) las nueve Gabi y yo _____ una ensalada fresca. (comer)

7. Nosotros _____ un postre: una tarta de manzana. (compartir)

8. Después Gabi y yo _____ en la terraza para conversar. (sentarse)

Let's review some adverbs and phrases that may be used for the exercises in this chapter.

ayer	*yesterday*	**varias veces**	*several times*
anteayer	*the day before yesterday*	**la semana pasada**	*last week*
anoche	*last night*	**el mes pasado**	*last month*
anteanoche	*the night before last*	**el año pasado**	*last year*
una vez	*once*	**el lunes pasado**	*last Monday*
dos veces	*twice*	**el martes pasado**	*last Tuesday*
esta mañana	*this morning*	**hace un año**	*one year ago*
esta tarde	*this afternoon*	**hace una semana**	*one week ago*

Y en tu caso, ¿verdadero (V) o falso (F)?

1. _____ Ayer me desperté temprano.

2. _____ La semana pasada hablé por teléfono con mis parientes.

3. _____ Esta mañana decidí ser más amable con mis vecinos.

4. _____ La noche antepasada escribí una carta para solicitar (*to apply*) un trabajo.

5. _____ El fin de semana pasado probé nuevos platos mexicanos.

6. _____ Por fin, hoy por la mañana recibí dos cheques por correo.

7. _____ Hoy pensé quedarme en casa para descansar.

8. **_____** Anteayer visité a mi familia.

9. _____ Anoche me acosté temprano.

10. _____ El año pasado estudié francés.

Verbs with spelling changes in the preterit

Verbs that end in -**car**, -**gar**, and -**zar** have a spelling change in the preterit in the **yo** form *only* to maintain the sound of the final consonant of the stem. Below are listed some frequently used verbs with this spelling change. Study these verbs before you read and answer the exercises in this chapter.

- ◆ Verbs ending in -**car** change **c** to **qu**

arrancar	*to start*	→ yo arran**qu**é
buscar	*to look for*	→ yo bus**qu**é
clarificar	*to make clear*	→ yo clarifi**qu**é
colocar	*to place*	→ yo colo**qu**é
dedicar	*to dedicate*	→ yo dedi**qu**é
desempacar	*to unpack*	→ yo desempa**qu**é
empacar	*to pack*	→ yo empa**qu**é
equivocarse	*to make a mistake*	→ yo me equivo**qu**é
explicar	*to explain*	→ yo expli**qu**é
pescar	*to fish*	→ yo pes**qu**é
sacar	*to take out*	→ yo sa**qu**é
tocar	*to touch*	→ yo to**qu**é

- ◆ Verbs ending in -**gar** change **g** to **gu**

apagar	*to turn off*	→ yo apa**gu**é
cargar	*to load*	→ yo car**gu**é
colgar	*to hang*	→ yo col**gu**é
encargar	*to order goods*	→ yo encar**gu**é
jugar	*to play*	→ yo ju**gu**é
llegar	*to arrive*	→ yo lle**gu**é
pagar	*to pay*	→ yo pa**gu**é
pegar	*to beat*	→ yo pe**gu**é

- ◆ Verbs ending in –**zar** change **z** to **c**

abrazar	*to hug*	→ yo abra**c**é
alcanzar	*to catch up*	→ yo alcan**c**é
almorzar	*to eat lunch*	→ yo almor**c**é
comenzar	*to begin*	→ yo comen**c**é
empezar	*to begin*	→ yo empe**c**é

lanzar	*to throw*	→ yo lancé
realizar	*to fulfill*	→ yo realicé
rezar	*to pray*	→ yo recé
tropezar	*to stumble*	→ yo tropecé

EJERCICIO
12·3

Traducción.

1. Yesterday I lost a gold ring and I looked for it in my apartment.

_____

2. I made a mistake.

_____

3. Where did I place my ring?

_____

4. I started to look for my ring in the living room.

_____

5. I prayed for a few minutes.

_____

6. Then I turned off the light and I left my living room.

_____

7. I took out a suit and a pair of pants from my car.

_____

8. Later, I hung them in a closet.

_____

9. Then I stumbled against a big suitcase.

_____

10. I touched something on the floor and I found my ring.

_____

11. I started to feel much better.

_____

12. Then I unpacked my suitcase.

_____

Preguntas personales.

1. ¿Empacaste tu ropa en una maleta el verano pasado para hacer un viaje?

   _____

2. ¿Colocaste la maleta en el maletero del auto de un amigo?

   _____

3. ¿Tocaste la guitarra, el violín o el piano ayer?

   _____

4. ¿Saliste temprano ayer de tu casa para ir al trabajo?

   _____

5. ¿Jugaste en uno de los equipos de deporte en tu escuela secundaria?

   _____

6. ¿Qué almorzaste ayer? ¿Y anteayer?

   _____

7. ¿Comenzaste un plan de dieta para mejorar tu salud?

   _____

8. ¿Dedicaste varias horas la semana pasada para aprender vocabulario en español?

   _____

Stem-vowel changes in the preterit tense

Change from i to y

In the preterit, -**ir** and -**er** verbs with a stem that ends in a vowel (e.g., **le-er, ca-er**), change **i** to **y** in the third person forms, both singular and plural. Note that in all the other forms the **i** takes a written accent.

leer *to read*	
leí	leímos
leíste	leísteis
leyó	leyeron

Verbs that end in -**uir** also change **i** to **y**, but there is no written accent in the **tú, nosotros,** and **vosotros** forms.

construir *to build*	
construí	construimos
construiste	construisteis
construyó	construyeron

contribuir	*to contribute*	**huir**	*to flee, run away*	
distribuir	*to distribute*	**incluir**	*to include*	

Ayer **contribuimos** a una campaña.
Yesterday we contributed to a campaign.

Vosotros **distribuisteis** los volantes en la tienda.
You distributed the flyers in the store.

El ladrón **huyó** de la casa de mi vecina.
The burglar ran away from my neighbor's home.

Review this list of common verbs that change **i** to **y** in the third person of the preterit.

INFINITIVE		YO	UD./ÉL/ELLA	UDS./ELLOS/ELLAS
caer	*to fall*	caí	cayó	cayeron
creer	*to believe*	creí	creyó	creyeron
oír	*to hear*	oí	oyó	oyeron
poseer	*to possess*	poseí	poseyó	poseyeron
proveer	*to provide*	proveí	proveyó	proveyeron

Some verbs do not follow the **i → y** change (e.g., **traer, atraer, distraer**). See Chapter 13 to read and learn the pattern of these verbs.

No **trajeron** los libros a la clase.
They did not bring the books to the classroom.

EJERCICIO 12·5

La naturaleza y accidentes. *Complete each sentence with the appropriate preterit tense form of the verb in parentheses.*

1. Anoche la lluvia y una tormenta _____ a accidentes de tráfico. (contribuir)

2. En casa, _____ nosotros muchos truenos. (oír)

3. La tormenta de vientos fuertes _____ un árbol en mi patio. (destruir)

4. Mientras manejaba, mi amigo _____ un ruido cerca de su auto. (oír)

5. Un peatón (*pedestrian*) _____ en medio de la calle. (caerse)

6. Un chofer de taxi salió del auto y _____ una botella de agua al peatón. (proveer)

7. Un desconocido salió de su auto también pero _____ del accidente. (huir)

8. Dos testigos (*witness*) _____ muchos detalles en su descripción. (incluir)

9. La policía _____ el mensaje del accidente a los periodistas. (distribuir)

10. Muchas personas hoy _____ la noticia en los periódicos. (leer)

EJERCICIO

12·6

¡Práctica! *First choose which of the verbs in parentheses best fits where in the sentence. Then complete each sentence with the appropriate form of the verbs in the preterit tense.*

Modelo: Yo _____ a mis amigos cuando ellos
_____ a mi casa. (abrazar / llegar)

Yo *abracé* a mis amigos cuando ellos *llegaron* a mi casa.

1. El partido _____ tarde porque _____ mucho ayer
por la tarde. (empezar / llover)

2. Un vendedor _____ una bolsa y yo _____ los
cacahuates. (lanzar / alcanzar)

3. Yo _____ cinco dólares y _____ los cacahuates con
Juan. (compartir / pagar)

4. Juan _____ su cámara y después _____ un video.
(grabar / sacar)

5. Yo _____ la cámara en un asiento vacío pero después (yo) no la
_____. (colocar / encontrar)

6. Juan _____ su cámara y por fin (él) la _____ debajo
del asiento. (buscar / descubrir)

7. En ese momento yo _____ mucho y también _____
que debo tener más cuidado con las cosas de mis amigos. (comprender / alegrarse)

8. Juan _____ mis disculpas (*apology*) y _____ varias
fotos de los jugadores. (aceptar / tomar)

9. El partido _____ tarde y Juan y yo _____ para ir a
un restaurante cerca del estadio. (terminar / salir)

10. Juan _____ el menú y él _____ tomar una sopa y
un plato de carne. (decidir / leer)

11. El camarero _____ el pedido en su libreta y _____
pronto la comida. (traer / escribir)

12. Después el dueño del restaurante _____ a un cliente y
_____ una botella de vino en su mesa. (saludar / colocar)

13. Yo _____ a bostezar y Juan _____ al camarero.
(empezar / llamar)

14. Juan me _____ a mí a cenar pero yo le _____
el dinero al camarero. (entregar / invitar)

Regular verbs in the preterit tense   **111**

Irregular and stem-changing verbs in the preterit tense

Previously you will have learned that in Spanish there are several verbs that are irregular in the preterit tense, and that these verbs follow certain patterns.

Irregular verbs in the preterit tense

Verbs that are irregular in the preterit follow a distinct pattern with either **u**, **i**, or **j** in the stem. You will find that for all three vowel changes the endings that follow the stem are the same: -**e**, -**iste**, -**o**, -**imos**, -**isteis**, -**ieron**. Note that none of the endings takes a written accent. Now let's review the three patterns.

- ◆ Verbs with **u** in the preterit stem

andar *to walk*	and**uv**-	anduve, anduviste, anduvo, anduvimos, anduvisteis, anduvieron
caber *to fit*	c**up**-	cupe, cupiste, cupo, cupimos, cupisteis, cupieron
estar *to be*	est**uv**-	estuve, estuviste, estuvo, estuvimos, estuvisteis, estuvieron
poder *to be able to*	p**ud**-	pude, pudiste, pudo, pudimos, pudisteis, pudieron
poner *to put*	p**us**-	puse, pusiste, puso, pusimos, pusisteis, pusieron
saber *to know*	s**up**-	supe, supiste, supo, supimos, supisteis, supieron
tener *to have*	t**uv**-	tuve, tuviste, tuvo, tuvimos, tuvisteis, tuvieron

The verb **haber** (there is, there are) also has **u** in the stem of the preterit: **hub**-.

Hubo una fiesta en la Casa Blanca para celebrar el Mes de la Hispanidad.	*There was a party at the White House to celebrate Hispanic Heritage Month.*

- Verbs with **i** in the preterit stem

hacer	*to do, make*	hic-	hice, hiciste, hizo, hicimos, hicisteis, hicieron
querer	*to want*	quis-	quise, quisiste, quiso, quisimos, quisisteis, quisieron
venir	*to come*	vin-	vine, viniste, vino, vinimos, vinisteis, vinieron

Note the spelling change, **c → z**, in the third person singular of **hacer**. The **z** in **hizo** maintains the soft **c** sound.

<blockquote>
Julio no hizo mucho ayer.   Julio did not do much yesterday.
</blockquote>

- Verbs with **j** in the preterit stem

atraer	*to attract*	atraj-	atraje, atrajiste, atrajeron, atrajimos, atrajisteis, atrajeron
conducir	*to drive*	conduj-	conduje, condujiste, condujo, condujimos, condujisteis, condujeron
decir	*to tell*	dij-	dije, dijiste, dijo, dijimos, dijisteis, dijeron
deducir	*to infer*	deduj-	deduje, dedujiste, dedujo, dedujimos, dedujisteis, dedujeron
distraer	*to distract*	distraj-	distraje, distrajiste, distrajo, distrajimos, distrajisteis, distrajeron
reducir	*to reduce*	reduj-	reduje, redujiste, redujo, redujimos, redujisteis, redujeron
traducir	*to translate*	traduj-	traduje, tradujiste, tradujo, tradujimos, tradujisteis, tradujeron
traer	*to bring*	traj-	traje, trajiste, trajo, trajimos, trajisteis, trajeron

EJERCICIO
13·1

Una visita a San Antonio. *Complete each sentence with the appropriate preterit tense form of the verb in parentheses.*

1. Ali y su esposo Juan _____ desde Tampa a San Antonio. (conducir)

2. Ali _____ las maletas. (hacer)

3. Por suerte, las dos maletas _____ en el maletero. (caber)

4. Ali y Juan _____ tiempo para salir temprano por la mañana. (tener)

5. Ellos _____ aquí a mi casa en San Antonio. (venir)

6. Ali, Juan, y dos amigos más _____ conmigo por dos semanas. (estar)

7. Ali _____ un regalo: un jarrón de flores. (traer)

8. Yo _____ el jarrón en la mesa del comedor. (poner)

9. Todos nosotros _____ por el Paseo del río San Antonio el domingo pasado. (andar)

10. Ali y Juan _____ disfrutar aquí dos semanas. (poder)

Una carta electrónica a un amigo. Traducción.

Dear Pepe,

Last week I told you that I love to read books about history. Yesterday I made a list of what I know about the history of Mexico. Then I went to the library and I was able to find a couple of interesting books in Spanish. I brought them home and put them on my desk. I started to check (revisar) the chapter titles. A few minutes later, Jaime came to visit me and we sat down to read. We found some difficult words. Unfortunately, my cat Lili distracted us a few times. This morning I had to make a decision. I am going to ask you a few questions about Spanish words and the themes of history.

See you later, Rocío

_____

_____

_____

_____

_____

_____

_____

_____

_____

_____

The preterit of **ser** and **ir**

The preterit conjugations of **ser** and **ir** are identical. The context around the verb forms indicates the meaning and which verb is being used.

ser to be	**ir** to go
fui	fui
fuiste	fuiste
fue	fue
fuimos	fuimos
fuisteis	fuisteis
fueron	fueron

¿No **fuiste** a Colombia el año pasado?	*Didn't you go to Colombia last year?*
Elena **fue** la directora de este colegio.	*Elena was the principal of this school.*
Jessi y yo **fuimos** a jugar golf ayer.	*Jessi and I went to play golf yesterday.*
Vosotros **fuisteis** amigos de verdad.	*You were truly friends.*

The preterit of dar and ver

Both **dar** and **ver** are irregular in the preterit. Both verbs take the endings of regular **-er** and **-ir** verbs; neither takes a written accent in the preterit.

dar *to give*	**ver** *to see*
di	vi
diste	viste
dio	vio
dimos	vimos
disteis	visteis
dieron	vieron

Traducción.

1. My friends and I went to a baseball game last night.

   _____

2. We saw the game on a big screen (**pantalla**) in the stadium.

   _____

3. I was one of the members of a baseball team in my high school.

   _____

4. We thanked (**dar las gracias**) Julio. He stood in (**ponerse en**) line for two hours in order to buy the tickets.

   _____

5. Did you (*sing., fam.*) see your favorite players?

   _____

6. Were you (*sing., fam.*) able to sit close to your friends?

   _____

7. I saw a beautiful young lady. She caught one ball without a glove!

   _____

8. Who was the big winner last night? I was! My favorite player won the game.

   _____

Y en tu caso, ¿verdadero (V) o falso (F)?

1. _____ Siempre fui un/a estudiante excelente.

2. _____ Jamás fui a Santander, en el norte de España.

3. _____ Hice todo mi trabajo ayer.

4. _____ Anoche vi un programa de noticias desagradables.

5. _____ Ayer estuve en una cola larga en un supermercado.

6. _____ Anteanoche traje a un amigo a mi casa.

7. _____ Esta tarde pude escuchar varios chismes (*gossip*) en la oficina.

8. _____ Traduje todas las oraciones del ejercicio anterior.

Stem-changing verbs in the preterit tense

You have reviewed stem changes in the present tense in Chapter 2. Most of the verbs have these stem changes only in the present tense. But the **-ir** verbs with stem changes in the present also have a few changes in the third person, singular and plural, of the preterit.

pedir *to ask for*	**dormir** *to sleep*
pedí	dormí
pediste	dormiste
pidió	**du**rmió
pedimos	dormimos
pedisteis	dormisteis
pidieron	durmieron

| Anoche Ramón **durmió** en la butaca. | *Last night Ramón slept in the armchair.* |
| Los zambrano nos **pidieron** ayuda. | *The Zambranos asked us for help.* |

For the following exercise you may want to review the list of commonly used verbs with the **e → i** stem change in the present tense in Chapter 2.

El apartamento de Nando y Lucho. *Complete each sentence with the appropriate preterit tense form of the verb in parentheses.*

1. Nando _____ para salir a una tienda. (vestirse)

2. Lucho, el compañero del apartamento, _____ las ventanas de la sala. (medir)

3. Nando _____ de su compañero de cuarto. (despedirse)

4. Él _____ las direcciones para llegar al centro comercial. (seguir)

5. En la tienda, Nando _____ la tela para las cortinas de las ventanas. (conseguir)

6. Él _____ un color claro. (elegir)

7. Nando _____ un descuento del diez por ciento a la vendedora. (pedir)

Verbs that change meaning in the preterit

Probably you have studied the verbs in Spanish that have different meanings according to whether they are used in the present or the preterit. This change in meaning in the preterit usually indicates that actions took place at a specific time. Some of these verbs include a negative word.

	PRESENT	PRETERIT
conocer	*to know*	*to meet*
	Conozco a Juan.	**Conocimos** a Pilar ayer.
	I know Juan.	*We met Pilar yesterday.*
poder	*to be able to do*	*to manage*
	Marisa **puede** traducir esta oración.	Ustedes **pudieron** ganar el partido de futbol.
	Marisa can translate this sentence.	*You managed to win the football game.*
no poder	*not be able to do*	*to fail to do*
	El testigo **no puede** hablar ahora.	El detective **no pudo** encontrar los documentos.
	The witness cannot speak now.	*The detective failed to find the documents.*
querer	*to want*	*to try*
	Quiero salir ya.	Ellos **quisieron** ir a California.
	I want to leave now.	*They tried to go to California.*
no querer	*not to want*	*to refuse*
	No quiere dibujar.	**No quise** hacer este trabajo.
	He does not want to draw.	*I refused to do this work.*
saber	*to know*	*to find out*
	Todos ellos **saben** la respuesta.	¿Cuándo **supieron** Uds. la noticia?
	They all know the answer.	*When did you find out the news?*

Traducción.

Last week I found a letter in my grandmother's trunk (**baúl**). Inside the envelope I saw ten old gold coins. I can understand messages in Spanish, English, and French but not in German. A few weeks ago I met Hans, a neighbor, and he is from Germany. I tried to ask Hans a few questions. Hans cannot help me because I found out yesterday that he is on vacation. I want to know the details of this mysterious letter. I do not want to talk about this letter with friends or members of my family. I do not want to give the gold coins to anyone.

_____

_____

_____

_____

_____

_____

El trabajo de mi oficina. *First choose the verb in parentheses that best fits each sentence. Then complete the sentence with the appropriate form of this verb in the preterit.*

Modelo: La vendedora _____ la atención de todos los clientes en la tienda. (caber / atraer)

La vendedora _atrajo_ la atención de todos los clientes en la tienda.

1. Yo no _____ salir temprano de casa hoy para ir a la oficina. (querer / venir)

2. Mi jefe _____ café y dulces para todos los empleados. (traer / distraer)

3. Paula _____ cinco libras de peso y no comió los dulces. (deducir / reducir)

4. _____ una reunión a las diez en la oficina. (hacer / haber)

5. Todos los empleados _____ en la reunión por dos horas. (andar / estar)

6. José Luis _____ participar y explicar las nuevas reglas para los empleados. (poder / poner)

7. Noemí _____ el documento del inglés al español. (conducir / traducir)

8. Todos nosotros _____ los nuevos productos en una pantalla en la oficina. (dar / ver)

The imperfect tense

The indicative imperfect tense in Spanish is used to communicate actions that happened in the past. Here we first review the imperfect tense and its uses, and then the use of the imperfect and the preterit in the same sentence. You may want to review Chapters 12 and 13, which include the uses and the conjugations of the preterit.

The imperfect tense is used to indicate actions, events, or situations that took place at a nonspecific time, or that happened several times or continuously in the past.

Camila **visitaba** a su familia en Colombia.	*Camila used to visit her family in Colombia.*
Su familia **vivía** cerca de Cali.	*Her family lived near Cali.*

Now, let's review the three conjugations of regular verbs in the imperfect tense.

Regular verbs in the imperfect

Almost all Spanish verbs are regular in the imperfect tense. To form the imperfect, drop the infinitive endings **-ar**, **-er**, or **-ir** and add the following endings:

-ar verbs: **-aba, -abas, -aba, -ábamos, -ábais, -aban**

-er verbs: **-ía, -ías, -ía, -íamos, -íais, -ían**

-ir verbs: **-ía, -ías, -ían, -íamos, -íais, -ían**

contar *to count, tell*	**vender** *to sell*	**abrir** *to open*
cont**aba**	vend**ía**	abr**ía**
cont**abas**	vend**ías**	abr**ías**
cont**aba**	vend**ía**	abr**ía**
cont**ábamos**	vend**íamos**	abr**íamos**
cont**ábais**	vend**íais**	abr**íais**
cont**aban**	vend**ían**	abr**ían**

Note that the **nosotros** and **vosotros** forms of -**ar** verbs take a written accent. The endings in -**er** and -**ir** verbs are the same throughout, and they all take a written accent.

Irregular verbs in the imperfect

Only three verbs are irregular in the imperfect tense: **ser**, **ir**, and **ver**.

ser to be	**ir** to go	**ver** to see
era	iba	veía
eras	ibas	veías
era	iba	veía
éramos	íbamos	veíamos
erais	ibais	veíais
eran	iba	veían

Los hábitos de Lulú. *Complete each sentence with the appropriate imperfect tense form of the verb in parentheses.*

1. Lulú y tú (*pl.; fam.*) casi siempre _____ a pasear los domingos cerca de tu casa. (ir)

2. Casi todos los días de la semana Lulú _____ muy tarde. (despertarse)

3. Sin embargo, ella _____ todos los días al trabajo. (ir)

4. Lulú y su hermana Alina _____ juntas. (vivir)

5. Lulú y yo _____ muy buenas amigas. (ser)

6. ¡Qué pena! Muchas veces las compañeras de trabajo _____ el cansancio en su cara. (ver)

7. A menudo Lulú _____ el pelo desarreglado. (llevar)

8. A veces, también ella _____ la camisa al revés (*inside out*). (ponerse)

9. En aquellos días yo _____ mucha pena por ella. (sentir)

10. Ella no _____ dormir porque _____ de insomnio. (poder, padecer)

11. Todos nosotros en la tienda _____ los problemas de Lulú. (conocer)

12. ¡Todos sus colegas _____ regalarle un despertador! (querer)

13. ¿Esto _____ una buena idea para un buen regalo o para una broma? (ser)

14. No, yo _____ que algunos _____ reírse de Lulú. (saber, querer)

Uses of the imperfect tense

The imperfect tense is used to express the following:

- A customary or habitual action, or an action that used to happen often in the past; the English equivalent is *used to* or *would*.

Nina **nadaba** en la piscina **los sábados**.	*Nina used to swim in the pool on Saturdays.*
Lisa **acompañaba** a Nina **a menudo**.	*Lisa would go often with Nina.*

- An action, a situation that was happening or was in progress in the past. There is no reference to when the action began or ended. English uses the verb *to be* + the gerund (*-ing* form of the verb) to translate this sense of the imperfect. Adding *-ing* to a verb in English indicates an action in progress.

Los chicos **jugaban** en el parque.	*The children were playing in the park.*

- A description of people, things, or events in the past

Ali **tenía** el pelo largo y los ojos verdes.	*Ali had long hair and green eyes.*
Las calles **estaban** resbalosas.	*The streets were slippery.*
El concierto **incluía** dos orquestas cubanas.	*The concert included two Cuban orchestras.*

- The time of day, the day of the week, or a date in the past

Eran las cuatro de la tarde.	*It was four o'clock in the afternoon.*
La reunión siempre **era los lunes**.	*The meeting was always on Monday.*
Era el primero de mayo.	*It was the first of May.*

- The age of a person or animal

Pablo **tenía cuarenta años**.	*Pablo was forty years old.*
Mi gato **tenía dos años**.	*My cat was two years old.*

- A state of mind in the past with **creer**, **pensar**, **querer**, **esperar**, or **saber**

Yo **pensaba** en ti todos los días.	*I used to think about you every day.*
Queríamos una casa con tres baños.	*We wanted a home with three bathrooms.*
Esperábamos el autobús cerca de mi casa.	*We used to wait for the bus near my house.*
Sabías que tenías problemas.	*You knew you had problems.*

- A physical sensation with **doler**, **sentir**, or **molestar**

Le **dolía la cabeza**.	*He had a headache.*
No **se sentía** bien.	*He did not feel well.*
¿Te **molestaba** el ruido?	*Did the noise bother you?*

Traducción.

1. When I was sixteen years old I used to live in a small town.

_____

2. My brother and I would run to a lake near our home.

_____

3. During the summer many of our friends used to swim in the lake.

_____

4. The lake was beautiful but the water was always cold.

_____

5. I always wanted to sleep under a tree.

_____

6. I felt comfortable and safe there.

_____

7. My brother and I always wanted to enjoy a long and delightful summer.

_____

Mi familia y yo. _First read the sentences. Then choose the letter that indicates the rule for the use of the imperfect tense._

1. _____ Mi primo Alberto siempre salía temprano por la mañana.

   a. a physical sensation

2. _____ Se despertaba temprano porque le dolía la espalda.

   b. a habitual action

3. _____ Era alto, tenía arrugas (_wrinkle_) en la cara y también era calvo (_bald_).

   c. a description

4. _____ Sal, mi hermano, quería una casa lejos de la ciudad.

   d. a person's age

5. _____ También deseaba comprar un auto nuevo.

   e. a state of mind in the past

6. _____ Sus hijas gemelas, Lola y Sarita, tenían 25 años en el año 2010.

7. _____ Mis tíos eran muy amables.

8. _____ Yo tenía dolor de cabeza.

9. _____ Mis padres tomaban café con leche todos los días.

10. _____ Mis primos pensaban en mí.

Una descripción en el pasado. *Complete each sentence with the appropriate form of the imperfect of each verb in parentheses.*

Cuando Juan 1. _____ (tener) quince años, todavía

2. _____ (dibujar) monigotes (*doodle*) en el cuaderno en la escuela.

Juan 3. _____ (ir) a casa y no 4. _____ (hacer) la

tarea. Su habitación 5. _____ (tener) dos ventanas y

6. _____ (haber) periódicos viejos en el piso. Cuando Juan

7. _____ (entrar) a su dormitorio, 8. _____

(escuchar) canciones, 9. _____ (ver) programas en la tele y

10. _____ (leer) las tiras cómicas (*comic strip*) en los periódicos. Juan

11. _____ (querer) resolver todos los problemas del mundo y

12. _____ (pensar) que la risa era la solución de muchos problemas.

¡Qué optimista 13. _____ (ser) Juan!

Phrases used with the imperfect

Previous examples included phrases that gave the context for the use of the imperfect. These phrases describe the frequency of repetitive and ongoing past actions and nonspecific time.

VOCABULARIO

You will use some of these expressions in the exercise that follows.

a menudo	*often*	**muchas veces**	*many times*
a veces	*sometimes*	**toda la vida**	*all one's life*
cada día	*every day*	**todas las semanas**	*every week*
cada año	*every year*	**todo el día**	*all day*
con frecuencia	*frequently*	**todos los días**	*every day*
en aquella época	*at that time*	**todo el tiempo**	*all the time*
en aquellos tiempos	*at that time*	**todos los años**	*every year*
frecuentemente	*frequently*	**varias veces**	*several times*
generalmente	*usually*	**varios días**	*several days*

Traducción.

1. My parents and I usually visited several cities in the United States when I was a young girl.

   _____

2. Every year we traveled to places like Fresno, St. Augustine, and other cities.

   _____

3. Many times my father rented a big car.

   _____

4. In those days I loved to stay a couple of days in different cities.

   _____

5. Sometimes I met new friends like Fernando.

   _____

6. Every week I wanted to talk to Fernando.

   _____

7. He was so funny! Several times I wrote his name and drew a heart on a piece of paper.

   _____

8. Fernando used to send me many letters.

   _____

9. I always felt happy reading his letters.

   _____

10. Fernando and I got married and now we remember those days when we were young.

   _____

Using the imperfect and the preterit in one sentence

The imperfect and the preterit are often used together in one sentence: the imperfect provides background information and describes a situation, wherever the preterit narrates an event. Usually the preterit is used for an action that interrupts an ongoing (imperfect tense) action.

Dormíamos.	*We were sleeping.*
El ladrón rompió la ventana.	*The burglar broke the window.*

Now let's combine the two actions in one sentence:

Dormíamos cuando el ladrón rompió la ventana.

Below are further examples of the preterit and the imperfect together in a sentence.

El policía **caminaba** cuando **oyó** un ruido. *The policeman was walking when he heard a noise.*

Mientras Eli **dormía**, el teléfono **sonó**. *While Eli was sleeping the phone rang.*

¿Quién no **quería** comer cuando **sirvieron** la cena? *Who did not want to eat when they served dinner?*

Traducción.

1. He interrupted me while I was talking.

_____

2. It was four o'clock when Rosa and I met at the florist (**floristería**).

_____

3. The car broke down while I was driving to the train station.

_____

4. You (*sing., fam.*) were still waiting for your friends when they came one hour late.

_____

5. Dr. Ruiz was with me when another patient screamed in the hallway (**pasillo**).

_____

6. Luis was reading a magazine when his brother called him.

_____

7. My friends were listening to a song when the doorbell rang.

_____

8. Who came to talk to Alex while he was in his office?

_____

Los problemas de la vida. Traducción. *Use the words in the* **Vocabulario útil** *for your translation.*

VOCABULARIO ÚTIL

annoying	**fastidioso, -a**	*pedestrian*	**el peatón / la peatona**
euphoric	**optimista**	*such bad luck!*	**¡qué mala suerte!**
holiday	**el día feriado**	*traffic lights*	**el semáforo**
luckily	**por suerte**	*to snore*	**roncar**
news	**las noticias**	*to stretch*	**estirar**
Oh, my God!	**¡Ay, Dios mío!**	*to yawn*	**bostezar**

This morning I woke up late. I yawned many times, I was happy, I felt optimistic. Then I opened the window in my bedroom and stretched my arms. The traffic lights were not working. Luckily, there was not much traffic on the street and I saw very few pedestrians. I went out to pick up my newspaper. I did not open it. I did not read the horrible news. I went to the kitchen and prepared my breakfast. I wanted to sleep and snore. Suddenly the alarm clock went off and I woke up. Oh, my God! It was not Saturday, not Sunday. It was not a holiday. Such bad luck! It was a dream.

_____

_____

_____

_____

_____

_____

_____

_____

The future tense

·15·

As you have learned, the future is a simple tense in Spanish. Unlike its English equivalent, it does not include an auxiliary verb such as *will* or *shall*. The future tense indicates and describes actions or events that will take place at some future date.

Algún día mis padres **vivirán** conmigo.	*Some day my parents will live with me.*
Leeré mi horóscopo mañana.	*I shall read my horoscope tomorrow.*
Regresaremos el mes que viene.	*We will come back next month.*

Regular verbs in the future tense

In Spanish most verbs are regular in the future tense. The endings are the same for all three conjugations: -é, -ás, -á, -emos, -éis, -án. They are added to the full infinitive. Remember that all endings, except the **nosotros** form, carry a written accent.

hablar *to speak*	**comer** *to eat*	**abrir** *to open*
hablar**é**	comer**é**	abrir**é**
hablar**ás**	comer**ás**	abrir**ás**
hablar**á**	comer**á**	abrir**á**
hablar**emos**	comer**emos**	abrir**emos**
hablar**éis**	comer**éis**	abrir**éis**
hablar**án**	comer**án**	abrir**án**

Me **llevarán** a tu oficina y **hablaremos**.	*They will take me to your office and we will talk.*
¿Dónde **comeremos** el sábado?	*Where will we eat on Saturday?*
Abrirás la carta en tu correo electrónico.	*You will open the letter in your electronic mail.*

The word *will* in English may indicate either an action in the future or someone's willingness or eagerness to do something. In Spanish the future tense is not used to express intent; for this, Spanish uses **querer** + an infinitive.

¿**Quieren** Uds. ayudar al candidato?	*Will they help the candidate?*
Queremos ayudar, claro que sí.	*We will help, of course.*

You may want to review Chapter 4 for expressions that are used to indicate or pinpoint when an action will take place in the future.

EJERCICIO
15·1

Y en tu caso, ¿verdadero (V) o falso (F)?

1. _____ Recibiré mi salario este fin de semana.

2. _____ Votaré en las próximas elecciones presidenciales.

3. _____ Mi equipo de fútbol favorito perderá este año.

4. _____ Gastaré menos dinero y ahorraré más.

5. _____ Subiré las escaleras y no usaré el ascensor para hacer ejercicio.

6. _____ Mañana decidiré los planes para mis vacaciones.

7. _____ De ahora en adelante veré el programa «La ruleta de la suerte» en español.

8. _____ Practicaré el español con un amigo.

9. _____ Correré cinco millas este fin de semana.

10. _____ El sábado que viene descansaré todo el día.

EJERCICIO
15·2

El pronóstico del tiempo. *Complete each sentence with the appropriate future tense form of the verb in parentheses.*

1. Mañana _____ a caer mucha agua en nuestra ciudad. (empezar)

2. El sábado no _____ un día soleado. (ser)

3. La temperatura _____ a 90 grados. (bajar)

4. Una tormenta _____ muchos árboles en nuestra área. (destruir)

5. La meteoróloga _____ los mapas en la pantalla. (mostrar)

6. Los televidentes _____ los nuevos pronósticos de la tormenta. (oír)

7. Un satélite no _____ en el Océano Atlántico. (caer)

8. Los bañistas no _____ hacer surfing en las playas. (deber)

9. Los agentes de la policía _____ a la comunidad. (proteger)

10. El martes _____ el tiempo. (mejorar)

Preguntas personales.

1. ¿Dónde celebrarás tu próximo cumpleaños?

_____

2. ¿A quiénes invitarás para celebrar tu cumpleaños?

_____

3. Imagina que tus amigos te regalarán doscientos dólares. ¿Qué comprarás con el dinero?

_____

4. ¿Cuántos años cumplirás este año?

_____

5. ¿Qué harás el fin de semana que viene?

_____

6. Y por último, ¿adónde irás de vacaciones el verano próximo?

_____

Irregular verbs in the future tense

The irregular verbs in the future are grouped into three categories according to the stem change. The endings are the same as for regular verbs, but are added to the irregular stem rather than the full infinitive.

- ◆ The stem drops the vowel of the infinitive and the endings are added to the irregular stem.

caber *to fit*	**cabr-**	cabré, cabrás, cabrá, cabremos, cabréis, cabrán
haber *to have (auxiliary)*	**habr-**	habré, habrás, habrá, habremos, habréis, habrán
poder *to be able to*	**podr-**	podré, podrás, podrá, podremos, podréis, podrán
querer *to want*	**querr-**	querré, querrás, querrá, querremos, querréis, querrán
saber *to know*	**sabr-**	sabré, sabrás, sabrá, sabremos, sabréis, sabrán

Remember that **haber** in an impersonal sense is used in the third person singular only.

¿**Habrá** una fiesta mañana?   *Will there be a party tomorrow?*
Habrá cien mil personas en el estadio.   *There will be one hundred thousand people in the stadium.*

◆ The infinitive stem drops the vowel of the infinitive and replaces the vowel with the consonant **d**; the endings are added to this irregular stem.

poner *to place, put*	**pondr-**	pondré, pondrás, pondrá, pondremos, pondréis, pondrán
salir *to leave*	**saldr-**	saldré, saldrás, saldrá, saldremos, saldréis, saldrán
tener *to have, hold*	**tendr-**	tendré, tendrás, tendrá, tendremos, tendréis, tendrán
valer *to be worth, cost*	**valdr-**	valdré, valdrás, valdrá, valdremos, valdréis, valdrán
venir *to come*	**vendr-**	vendré, vendrás, vendrá, vendremos, vendréis, vendrán

◆ The verbs **decir** and **hacer** are irregular; the stems are shortened and the endings are added to the changed stem.

| decir *to say, tell* | **dir-** | diré, dirás, dirá, diremos, diréis, dirán |
| hacer *to do* | **har-** | haré, harás, hará, haremos, haréis, harán |

EJERCICIO
15·4

En el circo. *Complete each sentence with the appropriate future tense form of the verb in parentheses.*

1. Un circo _____ aquí en esta ciudad por seis semanas. (estar)

2. Nosotros _____ la oportunidad de disfrutar ese espectáculo con muchos amigos. (tener)

3. Los boletos no _____ mucho. (costar)

4. Muchos payasos _____ reír a los niños y a las personas mayores también. (hacer)

5. Juan y Martín _____ temprano el domingo para sentarse cerca de los payasos. (venir)

6. Un mago _____ trucos (*trick*) con un sombrero y dos conejos. (hacer)

7. ¡Una domadora (*tamer*) _____ la cabeza en la boca de un león! (poner)

8. Mis sobrinos no _____ perderse ese espectáculo. (querer)

9. Ellos _____ la oportunidad de compartir ese día con sus amiguitos. (tener)

10. _____ mucha gente en el circo este domingo. (haber)

11. _____ la pena reír y disfrutar allí, en el circo. (valer)

Tu horóscopo. *Complete each sentence with the* **tú** *form of the future tense of the verb in parentheses.*

1. Cuidado: _____ visitar a tu médico. Es la época de la gripe. (deber)

2. _____ mucha suerte en el amor. (tener)

3. ¡_____ a la pareja ideal de tu vida! (conocer)

4. No _____ mucho dinero este mes. (ganar)

5. Pero luego, buenas noticias: _____ información de un viejo amigo. (encontrar)

6. _____ su recomendación para trabajar en una corporación con mucho éxito. (recibir)

7. _____ trabajar desde tu casa varios días a la semana. (poder)

8. _____ tiempo y dinero. (ahorrar)

9. Si vas al casino _____ mucho dinero en las tragamonedas (*slot machine*). (perder)

You may already know some of the verbs in the following Vocabulario. It shows verbs that are formed with a prefix (such as **com-**, **sos-**, **su-**, **dis-**) that precedes an irregular verb **tener**, **poner**, **hacer**, or **venir**. Note that some are used with a reflexive pronoun.

VOCABULARIO

abstenerse de	*to abstain from*	**mantener**	*to maintain*
atenerse a	*to depend on*	**obtener**	*to obtain, get*
componer	*to compose*	**oponerse a**	*to be opposed to*
contener	*to contain, hold*	**proponer**	*to propose*
convenir en	*to agree*	**rehacer**	*to remake*
deshacer	*to undo*	**reponer**	*to replace*
detener	*to arrest, detain*	**sostener**	*to hold up, support*
disponer de	*to have (at one's disposal)*	**suponer**	*to suppose*

Noticias de mi barrio. *Complete each sentence with the appropriate future tense form of the verb in parentheses.*

1. ¿_____ a las ideas de tus amigos? (oponerse, tú)

2. Mis amigos _____ un trofeo porque ganarán el torneo de tenis. (obtener)

3. Yo _____ de mucho dinero porque el caballo de mi abuelo ganó una carrera en Kentucky. (disponer)

4. Todos mis vecinos _____ que ganamos la lotería. (suponer)

5. Pero mi esposo y yo _____ el mismo estilo de vida: ahorramos, no gastamos mucho. (mantener)

6. Un ladrón robó a una pobre vecina. La comunidad _____ el dinero que ella necesita. (reponer)

7. Pronto el departamento de policía _____ a ese criminal. (detener)

8. Esta investigación _____ mucha información para ayudar a la policía. (obtener)

The future tense to express probability in the present

Another use of the future tense is to express wonder or probability at the present time. The equivalent in English is *I wonder, probably, must be, can be.*

¿Cuánto **costará** este sofá?	*I wonder how much this sofa costs.*
¿Qué hora **será**?	*I wonder what time it is.*
Serán las cuatro.	*It is probably four o'clock.*

Probabilidades. *Complete each sentence with the appropriate future tense form of the verb in parentheses. Remember that some of the verbs may be irregular.*

1. Julián _____ ya aquí en el aeropuerto. (estar)

2. Miriam, ¿ya _____ muy tarde para llamar a tu casa? (ser)

3. Mira, ¿cómo _____ esta persona? No recuerdo su nombre. (llamarse)

4. Esta señora _____ ser la madre de Mari. (poder)

5. ¿Qué opinas? ¿Ella _____ unos cincuenta años de edad? (tener)

6. Oye, hay un bolso en un asiento vacío. ¿A quién le _____ este bolso? (pertenecer)

7. ¿Cuánto _____ esta maleta tan grande? (costar)

8. _____ mucho en Tampa porque el vuelo está retrasado. (llover)

9. ¿Oyes gritos? Esas personas _____ mal. (sentirse)

10. Talvez porque ellos no _____ perder el vuelo de conexión en San Juan. (querer)

11. El auxiliar de vuelo, ¿nos _____ colocar esta maleta debajo del asiento? (dejar)

EJERCICIO
15·8

Un cuento de hadas. Traducción. *Use the words in the* **Vocabulario útil** *for your translation.*

VOCABULARIO ÚTIL

ballroom	**la sala de baile**	godmother	**el hada madrina**
by heart	**de memoria**	stepmother	**la madrastra**
carriage	**el carruaje**	stepsister	**la hermanastra**
Cinderella	**Cenicienta**	to drop	**dejar caer**
fairy tale	**el cuento de hadas**	wand	**la varita mágica**
glass slipper	**la zapatilla de cristal**		

Mila will be five years old soon. Tonight her grandmother Alina will read Mila's favorite fairy tale, Cinderella. Mila will fall asleep and she will dream of Cinderella. Mila knows this story by heart. Cinderella will help her mean stepsisters and she will follow the rules of her stepmother. Then her stepsisters will go to the ballroom in the palace. Luckily, Cinderella will have the help of her fairy godmother: with a magic wand she will create (**hacer**) a beautiful dress, a pair of glass slippers, and a luxurious carriage to go to the palace. Cinderella will meet the prince and will dance with him. At a quarter to twelve, she will go back home. Cinderella will drop (**dejar**) one of her glass slippers. And then the prince will find her and they will get married.

_____

_____

_____

_____

_____

_____

·16· The conditional tense

You probably have studied the conditional tense in Spanish. It is a simple tense: it does not need an auxiliary verb, unlike the English *would*, as the following examples show.

Carlos **estudiaría** varios idiomas.	*Carlos would study several languages.*
Yo **pintaría** las paredes con un color claro.	*I would paint the walls with a light color.*
Miguel y Marcos **perderían** el vuelo.	*Miguel y Marcos would miss the flight.*

Uses of the conditional tense

The conditional tense is used to express the following:

- A condition that would or might occur but has not yet been met

¿En qué estado de los EE.UU. **vivirías**?	*In which state would you live in the United States?*
Viviría en Texas porque me gusta la ciudad de San Antonio.	*I would live in Texas because I love San Antonio.*

- An action that would or might take place under certain circumstances or situations

Quizás Juan **estudiaría** alemán.	*Perhaps Juan might study German.*
No **compraría** este vestido aunque me gusta.	*I would not buy this dress even though I like it.*
Cocinaría en casa pero no tengo suficiente tiempo.	*I would cook at home but I do not have enough time.*

In the previous examples, the words **aunque** and **pero** are followed by the present tense to give an explanation—the reason why the action would or would not be completed. In some cases no reason is given: *I would not buy this dress even though I like it.*

Two reminders about translating the sense of *would* from English to Spanish:

- To convey the sense of *would* as *used to*, use the imperfect tense in Spanish.

  Yo **corría** a menudo por el parque.   *I often used to run around the park.*

- If *would* indicates *to be willing, to want*, use the preterit tense of **querer**.

  Luis no **quiso** correr hoy.   *Luis would not run today.*

Other uses of the conditional tense in Spanish are reviewed later in this chapter.

Regular verbs in the conditional tense

If you have reviewed Chapter 15 you will find that the future and the conditional tenses of all three conjugations have a lot in common: most verbs are regular, and the ending is added to the infinitive. The three conjugations have the same ending. Remember that all endings carry a written accent.

-**ar** verbs: -ía, -ías, -ía, -íamos, -íais, -ían

-**er** verbs: -ía, -ías, -ía, -íamos, -íais, -ían

-**ir** verbs: -ía, -ías, -ía, -íamos, -íais, -ían

Here are the full conjugations of the conditional tense.

hablar *to speak*	**comer** *to eat*	**abrir** *to open*
hablaría	comería	abriría
hablarías	comerías	abrirías
hablaría	comería	abriría
hablaríamos	comeríamos	abriríamos
hablaríais	comeríais	abriríais
hablarían	comerían	abrirían

Yo **vendería** mi casa pero me ofrecen muy poco dinero.   *I would sell my house but they offer me very little money.*

¿Dónde **compraríamos** la lavadora nueva?   *Where would we buy the new washing machine?*

Vivirías en un pueblo pequeño para disfrutar la belleza de la naturaleza.   *You would live in a small town in order to enjoy the beauty of nature.*

EJERCICIO
16·1

Y en tu caso, ¿verdadero (V) o falso (F)?

1. _____ Ahorraría más dinero para mi futuro.

2. _____ Pagaría la cena de todos mis amigos.

3. _____ Escribiría una novela histórica.

4. _____ Cambiaría mis costumbres, mis hábitos.

5. _____ Cantaría canciones mexicanas.

6. _____ Visitaría Colombia y Perú.

7. _____ Jugaría ajedrez con un amigo.

8. _____ Llegaría temprano a mi trabajo.

9. _____ Ayudaría a limpiar la casa.

10. _____ Bebería refrescos de dieta.

¿Qué pasaría? *Complete each sentence with the appropriate conditional tense form of the verb in parentheses.*

1. No _____ si la fecha es martes trece, un signo de mala suerte. (viajar, yo)

2. Somos perezosos, vagos, y _____ dormir hasta el mediodía. (preferir)

3. Mis amigas _____ a mi piso para tomar fotos de la ciudad. (subir)

4. Supongo que Uds. _____ juegos de mesa, ajedrez, parchís o dominó. (jugar)

5. Manolo y yo _____ los verbos irregulares del futuro y del condicional. (estudiar)

6. Los vecinos no _____ ruido. (oír)

7. Después Manolo _____ a nadar a la piscina aquí, en el edificio. (ir)

8. Yo no _____ más café si no puedo dormir por la noche. (beber)

9. ¿Y tú, _____ tacos con mucha salsa picante? (comer)

10. A Uds., yo les _____ ayuda para cocinar. (pedir)

Traducción. *Imagine you won one million dollars and a journalist asked you some questions.*

1. Would you spend all the money?

_____

2. Or would you save ten percent at least?

_____

3. What would you buy for your home?

_____

4. Would you help your family?

_____

5. Would you find another job?

_____

6. Would you donate some of your money to help your community?

_____

7. Would you enjoy (**disfrutar**) a few months at home?

_____

8. Would you travel to other countries?

_____

9. Would you like to ski in Colorado?

_____

10. Would you invite your friends to travel with you?

_____

Irregular verbs in the conditional tense

If you have reviewed the irregular verbs in the future tense in Chapter 15, you will find that the verbs that are irregular in the future are also irregular in the conditional. These verbs are grouped below according to the stem change. Note that the endings for all these verbs are the same throughout.

- ◆ The infinitive drops the **a**, **e**, or **i** from -**ar**, -**er**, -**ir** and the conditional endings are added to the irregular stem.

caber *to fit*	**cabr-**	cabría, cabrías, cabría , cabríamos, cabríais, cabrían
haber *to have* (*auxiliary*)	**habr-**	habría, habrías, habría, habríamos, habríais, habrían
poder *to be able to*	**podr-**	podría, podrías, podría, podríamos, podríais, podrían
querer *to want*	**querr-**	querría, querrías, querría, querríamos, querríais, querrían
saber *to know*	**sabr-**	sabría, sabrías, sabría, sabríamos, sabríais, sabrían

Remember to use the third person singular only in the impersonal use of **haber**.

¿**Habría** alguna posibilidad de comprar estos billetes?	*Would it be possible to purchase these tickets?*
Habría más o menos cien dólares en la billetera que encontré en la acera.	*There would be about one hundred dollars in the wallet that I found on the sidewalk.*

- Replace the final vowel of the infinitive with **d**. Add the conditional endings to this irregular stem.

poner *to place, put*	**pondr-**	pondría, pondrías, pondría, pondríamos, pondríais, pondrían
salir *to leave*	**saldr-**	saldría, saldrías, saldría, **saldríamos**, saldríais, saldrían
tener *to have, hold*	**tendr-**	tendría, tendrías, tendría, tendríamos, tendríais, tendrían
valer *to be worth*	**valdr-**	valdría, valdrías, valdría, valdríamos, valdríais, valdrían
venir *to come*	**vendr-**	vendría, vendrías, vendría, vendríamos, vendríais, vendrían

- The verbs **decir** and **hacer** are different; the stems are shortened and the conditional endings added to the irregular stem.

| decir *to say, tell* | **dir-** | diría, dirías, diría, diríamos, diríais, dirían |
| hacer *to do* | **har-** | haría, harías, haría, haríamos, haríais, harían |

EJERCICIO
16·4

Traducción.

1. It would be possible to meet our friends in San Juan.

   _____

2. I would put your big suitcase in the trunk.

   _____

3. Your suitcase would not fit in a seat of the car.

   _____

4. Would we be able to arrive at the airport early tomorrow?

   _____

5. I would say around (*a eso de*) five o'clock in the afternoon.

   _____

6. We would leave at three thirty but we live close to the airport.

   _____

7. We would not miss the flight to San Juan.

   _____

8. It would be worthwhile to enjoy one long weekend in Puerto Rico.

   _____

Posibilidades y decisiones. *Complete each sentence with the appropriate conditional tense form of the verb in parentheses.*

1. Jorge y su esposa Marilú _____ aquí a Alabama a visitarnos. (venir)

2. Ellos dos _____ en nuestra casa. (quedarse)

3. Yo _____ más almohadas en su habitación. (poner)

4. Mi madre _____ varios días si le pido este favor. (cocinar)

5. También nosotros _____ a otros amigos a nuestra casa. (invitar)

6. Eso _____ una sorpresa para Jorge y Marilú. (ser)

7. Esos amigos _____ que llegar antes de Jorge y Marilú. (tener)

8. ¿Quiénes no _____ disfrutar con sus amigos y recordar el pasado? (querer)

9. Yo _____ la verdad: es importante compartir con nuestros amigos. (decir)

10. Creo que _____ la pena pensar en la amistad y disfrutar la vida. (valer)

You may already know some of the verbs in the following **Vocabulario**, especially if you have read and studied the future tense in Chapter 15. These verbs are formed with a prefix that precedes the irregular verbs **tener, poner, hacer, venir**. Some are used with a reflexive pronoun, and a preposition may follow the verb.

VOCABULARIO

abstenerse de	*to abstain from*	**mantener(se)**	*to maintain*
atenerse a	*to depend on*	**obtener**	*to obtain, get*
componer	*to compose*	**oponerse a**	*to be opposed to*
contener	*to contain, hold*	**proponer**	*to propose*
convenir en	*to agree*	**rehacer**	*to remake*
deshacer	*to undo*	**reponer**	*to replace*
detener	*to arrest, detain*	**sostener**	*to hold up, support*
disponer de	*to have (at one's disposal)*	**suponer**	*to suppose*

Probabilidades. *First underline the verb for each question. Then write the appropriate form of the conditional tense for each answer.*

Modelo: ¿Tú _____ a las ideas de tus amigos? (<u>oponerse</u> / mantener)

              ¿Te opondrías a las ideas de tus amigos?

1. ¿Tú _____ otras canciones? (componer / obtener)

2. ¿Ustedes _____ más fama con esta nueva canción? (dispone / obtener)

3. ¿Esta competencia de música _____ ser muy difícil para ustedes? (poder / poner)

4. ¿Usted _____ de suficiente tiempo para llegar a su meta? (disponer / reponer)

5. ¿Tu canción _____ sentimientos del amor o nostalgia? (contener / detenerse)

6. ¿Quiénes _____ ser tus rivales como compositores? (poder / detener)

7. ¿Tú _____ a tus amigos el nombre de un cantante para cantar tu melodía? (mantener / proponer)

8. ¿Tú _____ el silencio para no comentar la canción? (reponer / mantener)

More uses of the conditional tense in Spanish

Some of these uses relate to past actions and others relate to the present.

- ◆ To express probability or speculation in the past, the equivalent of *could, must, would, probably, I wonder.*

Lila **me llamó** pero no **escuché** el teléfono. ¿A qué hora me **llamaría**?	*Lila called me but I did not hear the phone. I wonder what time she called me.*
Julio **salió** temprano esta mañana. ¿A dónde **iría** antes de llegar a la oficina?	*Julio left early this morning. I wonder where he went before he arrived to the office.*
Pablo **hizo** una cita con su médica. **Se sentiría** enfermo.	*Pablo made an appointment with his doctor. He must have felt sick.*

In the first two examples the verbs in the past tense clearly indicate that the actions happened in the past: **me llamó, escuché, salió**. The speculation is stated in the question that follows each example and the condition is not stated clearly. The third example states that someone made an appointment (**hizo**). **Se sentiría** expresses a possible reason why that happened.

If there is a need to express an action that would happen in the future from the perspective of the past, use the conditional.

Ayer **dijeron** que no **vendrían** hoy.	*Yesterday they said that they would not come here today.*

The next example does not state the condition clearly. The package might or might not have arrived, but the subject expresses what was known about the future.

¡Yo **sabía** que **llegaría** este paquete por correo!	*I knew that this packet would arrive by mail!*

◆ Express politeness or ask for advice

Luis, ¿**podrías** ayudarme a lavar esta ropa?	*Luis, could you please help me to wash these clothes?*
Sr. González, ¿**podría** Ud. decir cuánto cuesta este diamante?	*Mr. Gonzalez, could you please tell me how much this diamond is?*
Perdón, ¿cuál de estos dos anillos me **sugeriría** Ud.?	*Excuse me, which one of these two rings would you suggest?*

One of the uses of the conditional is to express a contrary-to-fact condition, a hypothetical statement that something is in fact not probable.

Si no **estuviéramos** enfermos, **iríamos** al cine.	*If we were not sick we would go to the movies.*
Compraríamos esta lámpara si **tuviéramos** el dinero suficiente.	*We would buy this lamp if we had enough money.*

In the two previous examples, **estuviéramos** and **tuviéramos** show the need for the imperfect subjunctive, a tense that is reviewed in Chapter 20.

EJERCICIO
16·7

Posibilidades en el pasado. *Fill in the blank with the appropriate letter of a sentence from the second column that indicates the probability that caused the action in the first column.*

1. _____ Quería tomar dos aspirinas.		a. No entendería las instrucciones.
2. _____ Se despertó a las cinco de la mañana.		b. Tendría dolor de cabeza.
3. _____ No hizo la tarea.		c. Querría ir al gimnasio temprano.
4. _____ Puso las toallas de baño en la cocina.		d. Necesitaría comprar vegetales y carne.
5. _____ No usó la tarjeta de crédito.		e. Tendría un dolor de muela.
6. _____ Fue al supermercado.		f. Tendría suficiente dinero.
7. _____ No contestó mi llamada.		g. Se equivocaría de lugar.
8. _____ Hizo una cita con una dentista.		h. No tendría suficiente gasolina.
9. _____ No usó su carro para ir a la oficina.		i. No los vería o estaría distraído.
10. _____ Preparó la cena a las once de la noche.		j. No escucharía el teléfono.
11. _____ No saludó a los vecinos.		k. Llegaría tarde a casa.
12. _____ Se despertó llorando y gritando.		l. Tendría una pesadilla (*nightmare*).

The present perfect and past perfect tenses

You probably have learned and used compound tenses in Spanish. A compound tense consists of an auxiliary verb and a participle. This chapter reviews two compound tenses: the present perfect and the past perfect.

The present perfect tense

In Spanish the present perfect is used to express actions in the past that continue in the present and to refer to a recently completed action. It is formed with the auxiliary (helping) verb **haber** in the present tense followed by a past participle. English uses a similar construction with a form of *to have* + a past participle: **He** + **hablado** (*I have spoken*).

Muchas personas **han llamado** a la estación de radio para dar su opinión.	*Many people have called the radio station to give their opinion.*
Yo **he enviado** mi carta al banco.	*I have sent my letter to the bank.*

First you must know how to conjugate the auxiliary verb **haber** in the present, and then how to form the past participle. Note that the **vosotros** form **habéis** takes a written accent.

haber *to have* (auxiliary)	
he	hemos
has	habéis
ha	han

Regular past participles

Past participles of regular verbs are formed as follows.

-ar verbs: drop the **-ar** ending and add **-ado**:	comprar	→ **comprado**
-er verbs: drop the **-er** ending and add **-ido**:	beber	→ **bebido**
-ir verbs: drop the **-ir** ending and add **-ido**:	vivir	→ **vivido**

The following examples show the formation of the present perfect in all three conjugations.

comprar *to buy*	**beber** *to drink*	**vivir** *to live*
he comprado	he bebido	he vivido
has comprado	has bebido	has vivido
ha comprado	ha bebido	ha vivido
hemos comprado	hemos bebido	hemos vivido
habéis comprado	habéis bebido	habéis vivido
han comprado	han bebido	han vivido

The past participle is invariable: that is, it remains the same, and does not agree in number and gender with the subject of the sentence.

Word order with the present perfect tense

The rules on correct word order apply to all compound tenses in Spanish. Remember that the auxiliary verb **haber** and the participle cannot be separated.

- In a direct statement of fact, the subject usually precedes the compound verb.

    Julita ha comprado dos camisas.   *Julita has bought two shirts.*

- In an interrogative sentence, the subject follows the compound verb.

    ¿Han probado ustedes el plato de camarones?   *Have you tasted the shrimp dish?*

- All object pronouns must be placed before the conjugated form of the auxiliary verb **haber**.

    Marta **nos ha pedido** un favor.   *Marta has asked us for a favor.*
    Ellos **me lo han llevado** a casa.   *They have brought it to me at home.*

- In a negative sentence, the negative word must precede the conjugated verb.

    No he comprado el regalo para Lucía.   *I have not bought the present for Lucía.*

- In a negative sentence that includes an object pronoun, the negative word precedes both the object pronoun and the conjugated verb.

    Ud. **nunca nos ha respondido**.   *You have never answered us.*

EJERCICIO
17·1

Traducción.

1. I have not spoken to my friends today.

   _____

2. My cousins have never been with me for two weeks.

   _____

3. Rita has showered but she has not washed her hair.

   _____

4. Have you (*sing., fam.*) sent me a message to go to a football game?

_____

5. Carla has never answered my question about her age.

_____

6. Has she ever told (**comentar**) you (*pl., fam.*) that she is younger than me?

_____

7. I have never understood why she is so secretive.

_____

8. We have not met before. It has been a pleasure.

_____

Uses of the present perfect

Let's review how the present perfect tense is used in Spanish.

- To indicate an action or something that happened in the past and bears relevance in the present or an action that continues in the present

Elías pensó en mudarse a Nueva York pero no **ha decidido** cuándo.	*Elías thought about moving to New York, but he has not decided when.*

In the next example, the verb **hemos venido** indicates that the action happened many times in the past and it is still happening in the present.

Nosotros **hemos venido** aquí de vacaciones por muchos años.	*We have come here for our vacation for many years.*

- To express a recently completed action

El vuelo **ha aterrizado** y podemos abordar el avión ya.	*The flight has arrived and we may board the plane now.*
Hemos usado la tarjeta de crédito porque la recibimos hoy por correo.	*We have used the credit card because we received it in the mail today.*

In Spanish, to express an action or something that just happened, you may use a form of **acabar de** + an infinitive, the equivalent in English of *has/have just* + a participle.

Acaba de llamar a Manuel.	*He has just called Manuel.*
Acabamos de terminar la tarea.	*We have just finished our homework.*
Mario **acaba de salir** del edificio.	*Mario has just left the building.*

Irregular past participles

Some past participles take a written accent to preserve the stress in pronunciation, or are irregular in their formation.

Past participles of -er and -ir verbs with stems that end in a vowel

When the stem of **-er** and **-ir** verbs ends with **a**, **e**, or **o**, a written accent is needed on the participle ending **-ído** to maintain the stress of the pronunciation. Verbs with infinitives that end in **-uir** need no written accent.

La soprano **ha atraído** al público para esta ópera.	*The soprano has attracted the public for this opera.*
La ciudad **ha reconstruido** esta carretera.	*The city has rebuilt this road.*

Below you will find a list of these verbs with the participle ending **-ído**. This list includes verbs and their compounds that are used frequently in Spanish.

atraer	*to attract*	**atraído**	**recaer**	*to suffer a relapse*	**recaído**
caer	*to fall*	**caído**	**reír**	*to laugh*	**reído**
creer	*to believe*	**creído**	**releer**	*to read again*	**releído**
desoír	*to disregard*	**desoído**	**sonreír**	*to smile*	**sonreído**
leer	*to read*	**leído**	**traer**	*to bring*	**traído**
oír	*to listen*	**oído**			

EJERCICIO
17·2

Y en tu caso, ¿verdadero (V) o falso (F)?

1. _____ Me han atraído las canciones de Shakira.

2. _____ Nunca he sonreído a mis vecinos.

3. _____ He releído varias veces las instrucciones para este ejercicio.

4. _____ He creído lo que dicen las noticias de hoy.

5. _____ He traído pescado para comer esta noche en casa.

6. _____ He desoído las sugerencias de mis amigos.

7. _____ Me he reído hoy con una película tonta y ridícula.

8. _____ He recaído en la gripe otra vez y tengo que descansar en cama.

9. _____ He oído varios chismes esta semana sobre una relación amorosa de dos amigos.

10. _____ He leído las noticias hoy en un periódico en la Internet.

More on irregular past participles

Remember that some common verbs have irregular past participles.

Eli no **ha abierto** la puerta hoy.	*Eli has not opened the door today.*
Ana **ha desenvuelto** el regalo que le di ayer.	*Ana has unwrapped the gift I gave her yesterday.*

You may review and use this list of irregular participles to understand and include the appropriate answers for the exercises that follow.

abrir	*to open*	abierto
componer	*to compose, write*	compuesto
cubrir	*to cover*	cubierto
decir	*to say, tell*	dicho
descomponer	*to break down*	descompuesto
describir	*to describe*	descrito
descubrir	*to discover*	descubierto
desenvolver	*to unwrap*	desenvuelto
deshacer	*to undo*	deshecho
devolver	*to return something*	devuelto
disolver	*to dissolve*	disuelto
encubrir	*to conceal, cover up*	encubierto
envolver	*to wrap*	envuelto
escribir	*to write*	escrito
freír	*to fry*	frito
hacer	*to do*	hecho
imprimir	*to print*	impreso
morir	*to die*	muerto
oponer	*to oppose*	opuesto
poner	*to place, put*	puesto
proveer	*to provide*	provisto
reescribir	*to rewrite*	reescrito
rehacer	*to redo*	rehecho
resolver	*to resolve*	resuelto
revolver	*to stir*	revuelto
romper	*to break*	roto
ver	*to see*	visto
volver	*to return*	vuelto

Remember that many adjectives in Spanish are actually participles of verbs.

Julia **ha sacado** los platos **rotos** del lavaplatos.

Julia has taken out the broken dishes from the dishwasher.

In this example you see the use of a participle following the auxiliary verb, **ha sacado**. This sentence includes the use of an irregular participle, **rotos**, from **romper**. A participle used as an adjective must agree with the noun in gender and number: **platos rotos**.

Una carta sentimental. *Write the appropriate form of the present perfect of the verb that appears in parentheses.*

Querida hermana Nina:

Martina me 1. _____(romper) el corazón. Yo 2. _____

(descubrir) que ella y yo no vamos a continuar nuestra relación amorosa. Martina ya le

3. _____(decir) a uno de nuestros amigos que mis padres

4. _____(oponerse) a nuestra relación, pero eso no es cierto. Martina

5. _____(encubrir) la verdad. Martina no me 6. _____

(devolver) el anillo de diamantes que le regalé. Ella me 7. _____(hacer)

muchas promesas falsas pero no las cumple. Nina, yo te 8. _____(escribir)

esta carta para decirte lo que siento dentro de mi alma. Yo no te 9. _____

(describir) todavía todo el amor que siento por Martina. Yo 10. _____

(poner) el retrato de mi novia Martina en una gaveta para poder olvidarla, ¡pero no puedo!

Ahora mismo yo 11. _____(volver) a poner su retrato aquí, en mi escritorio.

Yo 12. _____(deshacer) varias cartas que le escribí a ella. Siento tanto dolor

que no 13. _____(resolver) otros problemas que tengo ahora.

Un abrazo de tu hermano,

Luis

¿Qué ha pasado? *First choose the verb in parentheses that fits each sentence. Then complete each sentence with the appropriate present perfect tense form of the chosen verb.*

Modelo: El autor _____varias canciones esta semana. (composer / servir)

El autor *ha compuesto* varias canciones esta semana.

1. Los López _____su matrimonio con un divorcio amigable.
   (disolver / proveer)

2. Mis amigos _____mucho con un programa tonto en la tele.
   (oponerse / distraerse)

3. El perro de Paula _____hoy y su esposo le va a traer un gatito. (ver / morir)

4. Raúl _____calamares, pescado y papas para la cena. (revolver / freír)

5. El chico _____varias páginas de respuestas en esta impresora.
   (romper / imprimir)

6. Mi auto _____dos veces esta semana. (oponerse / descomponerse)

7. Yo no _____encontrar un buen mecánico para mi auto.
   (poder / revolver)

8. ¿Qué _____ nosotros? Que no hay buenos productos en esta tienda.
   (dar / ver)

9. El café está amargo porque tú no _____ el azúcar en la taza.
   (resolver / disolver)

10. ¿No _____ tú una solución para esos problemas? (resolver / proponer)

The past perfect tense

You may have learned that the past perfect is a compound tense. It therefore needs a form of the auxiliary verb **haber** in the imperfect followed by a past participle: **Yo había** + **salido** (*I had left*). Be aware that some textbooks in Spanish use the term pluperfect rather than past perfect.

These are the forms of the auxiliary verb **haber** in the imperfect.

haber *to have* (auxiliary)	
había	habíamos
habías	habíais
había	habían

Note that the first and third person singular forms are identical. The context will tell you which person is correct.

Reviewing regular past participles

Let's continue to review the formation of the past participle of regular verbs. The participles are used for all compound tenses; they do not change in number or gender. Here are examples of regular verbs in the three conjugations in the past perfect tense.

lavar *to wash*	comer *to eat*	salir *to leave*
había lavado	había comido	había salido
habías lavado	habías comido	habías salido
había lavado	había comido	había salido
habíamos lavado	habíamos comido	habíamos salido
habíais lavado	habíais comido	habíais salido
habían lavado	habían comido	habían salido

Word order in the past perfect tense

As already noted, the auxiliary verb **haber** and the past participle cannot be separated. The examples below show the required order of the words for the past perfect tense.

- Word order in a direct statement

  Marisa y Lola **habían vivido** en Madrid.   *Marisa and Lola had lived in Madrid.*

- Word order in an interrogative sentence

  ¿**Habías llamado** a tu hermano antes   *Had you called your brother before*
  de llegar aquí?   *you arrived here?*

- Word order in negative sentences

  No habíamos comprado el sofá en esta tienda. *We had not bought the sofa in this store.*

- Placing the object pronouns

  Yo **lo había llamado** antes de salir de casa. *I had called him before I left home.*

- Placing the object pronouns in a negative sentence

  Julián nunca me había invitado a su fiesta de cumpleaños. *Julián had never invited me to his birthday party.*

EJERCICIO 17·5

Y esto es ¿verdadero (V) o falso (F)?

1. _____ Los incas habían creado un sistema de comunicación por carreteras.

2. _____ Una científica francesa había descubierto la cura para la tuberculosis.

3. _____ Los conquistadores españoles habían llegado a las Américas antes del año 1500.

4. _____ Los astronautas norteamericanos habían entrado en órbita antes que los cosmonautas soviéticos.

5. _____ Antes de cumplir Bill Clinton sus sesenta años, el pueblo de los Estados Unidos lo había elegido como presidente.

6. _____ Salvador Dalí y Joan Miró habían visitado París al principio del siglo XX

   para ver las pinturas de los pintores de Francia.

7. _____ Los Estados Unidos se habían convertido en un imperio al principio del siglo XX.

8. _____ Miguel de Cervantes había publicado *El Quijote* antes de morir.

9. _____ Los experimentos científicos habían creado cura para todo tipo de cáncer en el siglo XX.

10. _____ Las novelas de Harry Potter habían creado ideas para películas.

Reviewing irregular past participles

Remember that in all compound tenses, the participle keeps the same form.

Julia **había vuelto** a la casa antes que yo. *Julia had returned home before me.*
Yo nunca **había visto** los cuadros de Dalí. *I had never seen Dalí's paintings.*
¿Quiénes **habían descubierto** este secreto? *Who had discovered this secret?*
Nosotros **habíamos puesto** la maleta en el maletero. *We had put the suitcase in the trunk.*

You may want to review the earlier list of irregular past participles before completing the following exercises.

¿Qué había pasado? *Complete each sentence with the appropriate form of the past perfect tense of the verb in parentheses.*

1. Mis amigos _____ alimentos a los vecinos que no los tenían. (proveer)

2. Yo les _____ todos los libros a mis amigos. (devolver)

3. Por suerte, los niños _____ mucho con los programas de la tele. (distraerse)

4. Rosa _____ las estrellas muy claras y brillantes en su telescopio. (ver)

5. Mi hermano _____ una copa de cristal en mi casa. (romper)

6. El auto de Lola _____ muchas veces. (descomponerse)

7. ¿Qué _____ Uds. antes de volver a casa? (hacer)

8. Mario mintió y nosotros _____ la verdad. (descubrir)

Uses of the past perfect tense

The past perfect tense in both Spanish and English refers to an action that *had occurred* prior to another action or condition. As you can see in the following example, before buying a new TV, the subject (**nosotros**) had saved the money—that is, someone *had* done this action.

Nosotros compramos un televisor nuevo porque **habíamos ahorrado** el dinero.	*We bought a new TV because we had saved the money.*

Adverbs are often used to indicate that one action preceded another. These adverbs, just like the pronouns and negative words, cannot be placed between the auxiliary verb and the participle.

antes	*before*	**nunca**	*never, ever*
aún	*still, yet*	**todavía**	*still, yet*
después	*after, later*	**ya**	*already*

Cuando llegamos al restaurante, mis amigos **ya habían comido** una ensalada.	*When we got to the restaurant, my friends had already eaten a salad.*
Yo **había llamado** a mis amigos **antes** de verlos en el restaurante.	*I had already called my friends before I saw them in the restaurant.*
Nunca habíamos ido a ese restaurante **antes**.	*We had never gone to that restaurant before.*

The completion of a past action may be implied without the use of an adverb. The following example does not indicate clearly *when* another action had or had not taken place prior to another action.

Jaime me **había contado** algunas noticias de   *Jaime had told me some news about*
su familia.   *his family.*

Mi educación y mis triunfos. *Complete each sentence with the appropriate past perfect tense form of the verb in parentheses.*

Antes de tener este auto deportivo, yo 1. _____(comprar) uno viejo. Yo nunca 2. _____(tener) la oportunidad de pedir un préstamo al banco. Mis padres ya me 3. _____(ayudar) para pagar las matrículas (*tuition*) para los cursos universitarios. Recuerdo que antes de terminar la escuela secundaria los autos deportivos y las motocicletas me 4. _____(interesar). Yo 5. _____(ver) las carreras de autos en Daytona por la tele. Pero mis padres 6. _____(negarse) (*to deny*) a entender mi pasión por los autos, especialmente mi madre. Antes de yo cumplir cinco añitos, ella me 7. _____(llevar) a museos interactivos para jugar pero también para aprender algo acerca de las ciencias. Pues bien, antes de cumplir mi madre los 60 años, yo le 8. _____(entregar) a ella mi diploma de ingeniería mecánica. Después de graduarme yo 9. _____ (recibir) una oferta de una industria automotriz. Pues ahora ya tengo el auto que siempre yo 10. _____(desear) y me encanta mi trabajo.

Boni y yo. Traducción. *Use the words in the **Vocabulario útil** for your translation.*

VOCABULARIO ÚTIL

amazing	**impresionante**	*to impress*	**impresionar**
ancestor	**el antepasado**	*to join*	**ingresar**
aristocrat	**el/la aristócrata**	*outgoing*	**extrovertido/-a**
to face	**enfrentar**	*to realize*	**darse cuenta de**
to find out	**enterarse**		

I had asked a friend of mine, Mario, a favor. I needed a letter of recommendation to join an exclusive and very expensive club. I had not told too many details to Mario. But I had told him that my ancestors were aristocrats and had a lot of money. When I met Boni I always had wanted to visit fabulous places and I had planned to introduce her to my friends in an impressive place, in that exclusive club. I had the impression that Boni was somewhat outgoing. After going out with Boni several times, I had realized that Boni is sincere. Therefore, I decided to face the truth: I do not have to impress anyone.

_____

_____

_____

_____

_____

_____

_____

_____

_____

The passive voice

As you know, there are two ways to communicate the passive voice in Spanish. These two forms are reviewed and explained in this chapter.

The active voice vs. the passive voice

A sentence in the active voice indicates that the subject—the agent of the action—performs the action (the verb). The sentence may include a recipient—an object or person that receives the action:

subject (the agent)+ verb+ object (what/who receives the action)

Mario Vargas Llosa escribió la novela.	*Mario Vargas Llosa wrote the novel.*

In the passive voice, however, the subject is *acted upon*. If the agent—the doer of the action—is mentioned, the preposition **por** is placed before the agent.

subject (receives the action) + verb + **por** + who/what performs the action

La novela fue escrita por Mario Vargas Llosa.	*The novel was written by Mario Vargas Llosa.*

In a sentence in the passive voice, the agent may be unknown or unspecified. The preceding example does show the agent, **Mario Vargas Llosa**. However, the next two examples in the passive do not specify *who* closed the door, or *who* introduced the writers:

La librería **fue cerrada**.	*The bookstore was closed.*
Los escritores **fueron presentados** ante el público.	*The writers were introduced to the public.*

Formation of the passive

The formation of the passive voice in Spanish is similar to that in English: (subject) + form of the verb **ser** + past participle + **por** + agent. This formation does not change from one tense to another. (You may want to review the list of irregular participles in Chapter 17.) In the following examples you will find the use of the passive voice in the different tenses.

PRESENT	La presidenta del comité **es elegida por** los miembros de su grupo.	*The president of the committee is elected by the group members.*
FUTURE	Estos documentos **serán impresos** por los empleados.	*These documents will be printed by the employees.*
PRETERIT	Las puertas no **fueron instaladas** por un grupo de carpinteros.	*The doors were not installed by a group of carpenters.*
PRESENT PERFECT	El documento para el divorcio **ha sido firmado** por dos abogados.	*The divorce document has been signed by two lawyers.*
PAST PERFECT	El proyecto de la universidad **había sido diseñado** por dos arquitectos.	*The university project had been designed by two architects.*

In the passive voice the past participle must agree in gender and number with the subject of the verb. This is the same form of the participle that we use for certain adjectives. You may review Chapter 3 for participles used as adjectives.

El nombre del ganador fue **anunciado** ayer.	*The name of the winner was announced yesterday.*
Las noticias habían sido **publicadas**.	*The news had been published.*
Los regalos de Mari fueron **envueltos** en la tienda.	*Mari's gifts were wrapped at the store.*
Unas notas fueron **escritas** en este papel.	*Some notes were written on this paper.*

The passive voice in Spanish is not used frequently in daily conversations, but it tends to appear in newspaper articles and on TV and radio.

Dos bancos **fueron asaltados** ayer.	*Two banks were robbed yesterday.*
Un sospechoso **fue interrogado** por la policía.	*Two suspects were interrogated by the police.*
Los candidatos **serán elegidos** mañana.	*The candidates will be elected tomorrow.*

EJERCICIO
18·1

Una feria popular. *Write the appropriate form of the participle of the verb that appears in parentheses. Attention: some participles are irregular.*

1. Las puertas de un parque fueron _____ a las ocho de la mañana. (abrir)

2. Unos loros de Centroamérica han sido _____ en esas jaulas. (traer)

3. Los dibujos de caricaturas fueron _____ por un personaje desconocido. (dibujar)

4. Los objetos de artesanía habían sido _____ en las calles principales. (vender)

5. Los carteles de la protesta serán _____ frente al ayuntamiento esta noche. (distribuir)

6. El plato típico de Perú, ceviche, será _____ en la Tercera Avenida. (preparar)

7. La fiesta de esta ciudad es _____ el 25 de mayo de cada año. (celebrar)

8. Algunos cantantes y guitarristas fueron _____ el año pasado. (invitar)

9. Esta celebración fue _____ por el ayuntamiento años atrás. (aprobar)

10. Muchos artículos típicos de Hispanoamérica serán _____ para decorar las calles. (donar)

EJERCICIO
18·2

La boda. Traducción.

1. The invitations had been sent.

_____

2. The invitations were made by some members of the family.

_____

3. The addresses on the envelopes were written by the bride's sister.

_____

4. A contract had been signed by the band.

_____

5. The menu was created by a Peruvian chef.

_____

6. The ballroom was decorated with many flowers.

_____

7. The day of the wedding was selected by the bride.

_____

8. The presents were sent by the friends of the groom and the bride.

_____

9. Champagne was served for a toast (**el brindis**).

_____

10. Many photographs were taken in the ballroom.

_____

The passive reflexive

Another way to express the sense of the passive voice in Spanish is the passive reflexive. It is important to understand the passive reflexive construction and its uses because it is used more frequently than the passive voice in everyday conversations in Spanish.

With the passive reflexive an action is performed, yet an agent—the doer of the action—is not stated. The reflexive pronoun **se** appears first and a conjugated verb follows. If a singular noun follows the verb, the verb is conjugated in the third person singular; the third person plural follows a plural noun.

PASSIVE REFLEXIVE, SINGULAR

se + verb (third person singular) + singular noun

Se recicla el papel aquí.	*The paper is recycled here.*
Se abre la oficina a las ocho de la mañana.	*The office is opened at eight in the morning.*
Se necesita un camarero en el restaurante.	*A waiter is needed in the restaurant.*

PASSIVE REFLEXIVE, PLURAL

se + verb (third person plural) + plural noun

Se cierran las puertas a las seis.	*The doors are closed at six.*
Se recogen las botellas vacías en el segundo piso.	*The empty bottles are collected on the second floor.*
Se aceptan los documentos en aquella ventanilla.	*The documents are accepted at that window.*

The passive reflexive is used in all tenses, but the construction does not change from one tense to another. The reflexive pronoun **se** appears in all tenses.

Se vendieron todas las copias de la novela.	*All the copies of the novel were sold.*
Se celebrará el aniversario de bodas de Ana y Paco aquí.	*Ana and Paco's wedding anniversary will be celebrated here.*
No **se habían escrito** estos libros para entretener a los niños.	*These books were not written to entertain the children.*

You may want to review the present perfect tense in Chapter 17 before completing the following exercises.

EJERCICIO
18·3

Comentarios en una reunión en la oficina. *Complete each sentence in the passive reflexive using the present perfect tense form of the verb in parentheses.*

1. _____las puertas ya. (cerrar)

2. No _____las notas de la reunión. (escribir)

3. No _____las reglas todavía. (leer)

4. _____los comentarios negativos aquí. (prohibir)

5. _____botellas de agua al frente de la cafetería. (vender)

6. No _____ este problema. (resolver)

7. No _____ tus sugerencias. (aceptar)

8. _____ los documentos por correo electrónico. (enviar)

9. _____ los arbolitos de navidad. (poner)

10. _____ la relación de amistad entre Juanita y yo. (romper)

¿Qué opinas, cierto (C) o no (N)?

1. _____ Se podía viajar en un avión a finales del siglo XIX.

2. _____ En esta época se fabrican muchos autos en Japón y Corea del Sur.

3. _____ Se habla más inglés que español en Chile.

4. _____ Ahora se usan los teléfonos para enviar fotos a la familia.

5. _____ Se habla solamente español en Francia.

6. _____ En diez años se descubrirán más soluciones para la salud de muchos individuos.

7. _____ Se puede encontrar casi toda la información necesaria a través de la Internet.

8. _____ En el futuro se podrá manejar todo tipo de auto sin usar gasolina.

Traducción. *Use the passive reflexive to translate each of the following sentences.*

1. How do you say "thanks" in French?

_____

2. Where do they sell toys?

_____

3. When will they raise (**aumentar**) the prices?

_____

4. Where do they buy books written in Japanese?

_____

5. What is spoken here at this store?

_____

6. When do they serve breakfast in the hotel?

_____

7. Where do they accept coupons for discount?

_____

8. How do you say "I am sorry" in Portuguese?

_____

Uses of the impersonal pronoun se

The reflexive pronoun appears in impersonal constructions (see Chapter 7) where the subject of the sentence is indefinite. It is used with the third personal singular of the verb. The impersonal in English is expressed with a subject—*people, they, you, we, one.*

Se comenta mucho acerca del divorcio de estos dos cantantes famosos.	*People are talking about the divorce of these two famous singers.*
Se dice que vale la pena dormir ocho horas cada noche.	*They say that is worthwhile to sleep eight hours every night.*
No **se debe** ir a una fiesta sin una invitación.	*You should not go to a party without an invitation.*
¿**Se puede** encontrar un hotel elegante aquí?	*Can one find an elegant hotel here?*

The next exercise offers you practice with the impersonal pronoun **se**.

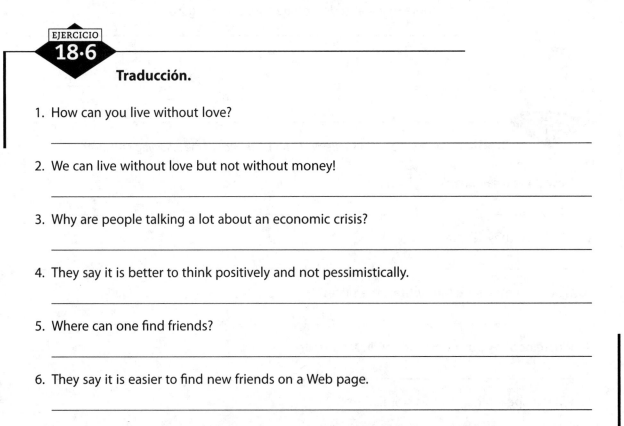

EJERCICIO
18·6

Traducción.

1. How can you live without love?

_____

2. We can live without love but not without money!

_____

3. Why are people talking a lot about an economic crisis?

_____

4. They say it is better to think positively and not pessimistically.

_____

5. Where can one find friends?

_____

6. They say it is easier to find new friends on a Web page.

_____

Una entrevista. Traducción. *Use the words in the* **Vocabulario útil** *for your translation.*

VOCABULARIO ÚTIL

coach	**el entrenador / la entrenadora**
to get used to	**acostumbrarse**
to maintain	**mantenerse**
Olympic Games	**las Olimpiadas**
to promise	**comprometerse**
schedule	**el horario**
self-confidence	**la confianza en sí mismo, -a**
stopwatch	**el cronómetro**
warm-up exercises	**los ejercicios de calentamiento**

—How is a swimmer trained to compete in the Olympic Games?

—Usually, she or he is trained by a professional coach.

—How many days a week?

—It is known that all athletes train six days a week and they rest for one day.

—But how many hours do they swim in a pool?

—Many hours, and they promise to rest and to sleep.

—What is expected from an athlete who wants to swim in the next Olympic Games?

—A lot is expected: to have self-confidence, to persevere, and to maintain himself or herself in good shape, physically and mentally.

—Is it necessary to have a daily schedule?

—Yes, it's needed in order to get used to a daily routine.

—Please, give me (*sing,. form.*) an example of a daily schedule.

—Of course. He/She gets out of bed early, then does warm-up exercises. A stopwatch is used to measure the time and the speed while he/she swims.

—Many thanks, and see you later.

_____

_____

_____

_____

_____

_____

The present subjunctive

You may have learned the conjugated forms of the present subjunctive and how to communicate with people who speak or have learned to speak Spanish. In previous chapters we have discussed tenses in the indicative mood. This chapter begins our review of the subjunctive mood.

The word *mood* describes the attitude of the subject. The indicative mood states or indicates certainty: something is real or certain.

Juan **sabe** que yo **vivo** en Madrid.   *Juan knows that I live in Madrid.*

The subject **Juan** in the main clause knows with certainty something about the subject of the second clause, **yo**. The same tense, the present indicative, appears in both clauses, which are connected with the conjunction **que**.

The next example shows a past indicative tense, the imperfect.

Julián **sabía** que **íbamos** a viajar a Ecuador.   *Julian knew that we would travel to Ecuador.*

The subjunctive mood, on the other hand, expresses uncertainty, something that is not known or will not happen for sure.

Yo espero que **vengas** mañana.   *I hope that you come tomorrow.*

In the first clause, **espero**, itself in the indicative, shows some uncertainty, a wish that something may be completed. In the subsidiary clause the verb **vengas** is in the subjunctive. Note that the conjunction **que** connects the two clauses.

The subjunctive mood is used more frequently in Spanish than in English. Therefore, we need to know and remember the situations where it is used, as in the following examples.

- Uncertainty

    Compraremos el auto aunque **cueste** mucho.   *We will buy the car even if it costs a lot.*

- Doubt

    Nosotros **dudamos** que Marta **venga** esta noche.   *We doubt (It is unlikely) that Marta will come tonight.*

- Demand

    Exigen que **llamemos** antes de las ocho.

    They insist that we call before eight o'clock.

- Desire, hope

    Julia y yo **deseamos** que **pases** un día feliz.

    Julia and I wish you a nice day.

    ¡**Espero** que **ganes** la lotería!

    I hope that you win the lottery!

- Emotions and feelings

    Ellos **temen** que tú **no vuelvas** mañana a casa.

    They are afraid that you won't come back home tomorrow.

    Yo **me alegro** de que Uds. **puedan** cenar conmigo.

    I am happy that you can dine with me.

- Indefinite, nonexistent person or thing in the subordinate clause

    Necesitamos **una secretaria que sea** bilingüe.

    We need a secretary who is bilingual.

    Quiero **un apartamento que tenga** una cocina grande.

    I want an apartment with a big kitchen.

    No conozco **a nadie que quiera** ayudar a esta comunidad.

    I don't know anyone who wants to help this community.

- Impersonal expressions with opinions and suggestions

    Es necesario que Uds. **firmen** esta carta.

    It is necessary that you sign this letter.

    Es posible que **llueva** esta tarde.

    (I think) It may rain this afternoon.

Formation of the present subjunctive

Most verbs in the present subjunctive are conjugated in the same way, including verbs that have stem changes in the present. Almost all stem-changing verbs in the present indicative have the same changes in the present subjunctive (see Chapter 2 to review stem-changing verbs).

To form the present subjunctive in the three conjugations of regular verbs, take the **yo** form of the present indicative, drop the -**o** ending, and add the endings of the present subjunctive as follows:

-**ar** verbs:	-**e, -es, -e, -emos, -éis, -en**
-**er** verbs:	-**a, -as, -a, -amos, -áis, -an**
-**ir** verbs:	-**a, -as, -a, -amos, -áis, -an**

bailar *to dance*	**beber** *to drink*	**escribir** *to write*
bail**e**	beb**a**	escrib**a**
bail**es**	beb**as**	escrib**as**
bail**e**	beb**a**	escrib**a**
bail**emos**	beb**amos**	escrib**amos**
bail**éis**	beb**áis**	escrib**áis**
bail**en**	beb**an**	escrib**an**

Here now are the present subjunctive conjugations of many familiar verbs.

destruir	*to destroy*	destruya, destruyas, destruya, destruyamos, destruyáis, destruyan
hacer	*to make*	haga, hagas, haga, hagamos, hagáis, hagan
querer	*to want*	quiera, quieras, quiera, queramos, queráis, quieran
salir	*to go out*	salga, salgas, salga, salgamos, salgáis, salgan
tener	*to hold*	tenga, tengas, tenga, tengamos, tengáis, tengan
ver	*to see*	vea, veas, vea, veamos, veáis, vean

From this, you see that the first and third person singular endings are the same. The –er and -ir verbs have the same endings in all forms. Only the **vosotros** form has a written accent. Of these preceding examples, you will see no stem changes in the first and second person plural forms of **querer: queramos, queráis**.

♦ Three other verbs make a stem change in the **nosotros** and **vosotros** forms.

mentir	e → i	**mintamos, mintáis**
dormir	o → u	**durmamos, durmáis**
pedir	e → i	**pidamos, pidáis**

You may want to review verbs with spelling changes in the present indicative tense for the **yo** form only in Chapter 2. These verbs end in -**cer**, -**ger**, -**gir**, and -**guir** in the present indicative. As you can see, **coger, conocer, dirigir**, and **distinguir** maintain these spelling changes in all persons, singular and plural, in the present subjunctive.

coger	*to take*	coja, cojas, coja, cojamos, cojáis, cojan
conocer	*to know*	conozca, conozcas, conozca, conozcamos, conozcáis, conozcan
dirigir	*to direct*	dirija, dirijas, dirija, dirijamos, dirijáis, dirijan
distinguir	*to distinguish*	distinga, distingas, distinga, distingamos, distingáis, distingan

Verbs with spelling changes in the present subjunctive

In Chapter 12 you reviewed spelling changes in the preterit for verbs that end in -**car**, -**gar**, and -**zar**. These verbs maintain this spelling change in the present subjunctive.

First, go to the **yo** form of the preterit indicative, drop the -**e** ending, and add the present subjunctive endings for -**ar** verbs already given: -**e**, -**es**, -**e**, -**emos**, -**éis**, -**en**:

INFINITIVE	PRETERIT	PRESENT SUBJUNCTIVE STEM
buscar	bus**qué**	**busqu-**
apagar	apa**gué**	**apagu-**
abrazar	abra**cé**	**abrac-**

Here are more examples of verbs with this spelling change in the present subjunctive.

abrazar	*to embrace*	abrace, abraces, abrace, abracemos, abracéis, abracen
apagar	*to turn off*	apague, apagues, apague, apaguemos, apaguéis, apaguen
buscar	*to look for*	busque, busques, busque, busquemos, busquéis, busquen
dedicar	*to dedicate*	dedique, dediques, dedique, dediquemos, dediquéis, dediquen
explicar	*to explain*	explique, expliques, explique, expliquemos, expliquéis, expliquen

llegar	*to arrive*	llegue, llegues, llegue, lleguemos, lleguéis, lleguen
pagar	*to pay*	pague, pagues, pague, paguemos, paguéis, paguen
sacar	*to withdraw*	saque, saques, saque, saquemos, saquéis, saquen
tocar	*to touch*	toque, toques, toque, toquemos, toquéis, toquen

Irregular verbs in the present subjunctive

There are a few verbs that are irregular in the present subjunctive. These are all verbs we use frequently in daily communication.

dar	*to give*	dé, dés, dé, demos, deis, den
estar	*to be*	esté, estés, esté, estemos, estéis, estén
haber	*there is, are*	haya, hayas, haya, hayamos, hayáis, hayan
ir	*to go*	vaya, vayas, vaya, vayamos, vayáis, vayan
saber	*to know*	sepa, sepas, sepa, sepamos, sepáis, sepan
ser	*to be*	sea, seas, sea, seamos, seáis, sean

Uses of the present subjunctive

As shown earlier in this chapter, in Spanish we use the subjunctive when there is a need to express advice and suggestions, demand and orders, desire and hope, doubt or uncertainty, feelings and emotions, requests and impersonal opinion.

The verb in the main clause, which expresses the advice, suggestion, desire, demand, is in the indicative. The subjunctive form appears in the subordinate clause, usually after the conjunction **que** (*that*).

Mi padre quiere que **yo prepare** la cena.   *My father wants me to prepare dinner.*

The main clause with the indicative **quiere** states a wish of the subject, **mi padre**. He expects that wish to be fulfilled by the subject in the subordinate clause, **yo**. This second clause does not state whether dinner will be prepared or not. In English the equivalent formation includes not a subjunctive form in the subordinate clause but rather an infinitive (*to prepare*) after the pronoun *me*.

If the subjects in the main clause and the subordinate clause are different, use the subjunctive in the subsidiary clause.

Yo necesito que **tú compres** el billete.   *I want you to buy the ticket.*

If the subject is the same in both clauses, use the infinitive in the subsidiary clause. Note that there is no need for **que** in this case.

Yo necesito comprar el billete.   *I need to buy the ticket.*

In the first example **yo** is the subject of the main clause, **tú** is the subject of the subordinate clause. There is no subject other than **yo** in the second example.

The following lists give you verbs that frequently precede sentences with the subjunctive.

- ◆ Verbs to express advice and suggestions

aconsejar	*to advise, give advice to someone*
insistir en	*to insist*
preferir	*to prefer*
recomendar	*to advise*
sugerir	*to suggest*

Yo **te aconsejo** que **tú firmes** ahora.	*I advise you to sign now.*
Joaquín **insiste en** que **tú vayas** a su casa.	*Joaquin insists that you go to his home.*
Nosotros **preferimos** que los chicos **vean** esta película.	*We prefer that the children watch this movie.*
Ellos **sugieren** que **lleguemos** temprano.	*They suggest that we arrive early.*

- ◆ Verbs that express orders and demands

decir	*to tell, order*
exigir	*to require, call for, demand*
mandar	*to tell, order, give orders*
permitir	*to allow, permit*
prohibir	*to prohibit, forbid*

Alina **dice** que **prepares** la merienda ahora.	*Alina says (orders) that you should prepare the snack now.*
La dueña **exige** que yo **pague** mi alquiler el día primero de cada mes.	*The owner requires that I pay my rent the first day of every month.*
El sargento **manda** que **abras** las puertas.	*The sergeant orders you to open the doors.*
La ley **prohíbe** que ustedes **fumen** cigarrillos aquí.	*The law prohibits smoking (that you smoke) here.*

- ◆ Verbs that express desire, hope

desear	*to wish*
esperar	*to hope, expect*
querer	*to want, expect*

Doris **desea** que Uds. **viajen** con ella.	*Doris wants you to travel with her.*
Yo **espero** que mi hermana **viva** conmigo.	*I hope that my sister will live with me.*
El maestro **quiere** que los chicos **aprendan** español.	*The teacher wants the children to learn Spanish.*

The interjection **ojalá** expresses hope, desire, wish; therefore, the subjunctive mood follows this interjection, which is used very frequently in daily communication.

ojalá (que)	*I wish that, I hope that, God willing*
¡Ojalá puedas ganar!	*I hope that you win!*
Ojalá que no **nieve** esta noche.	*I hope it doesn't snow tonight.*
Ojalá que ganemos este partido.	*God willing, we'll win this game.*

En el teatro. *Complete each sentence with the appropriate form of the present subjunctive of the verb in parentheses.*

1. Espero que Uds. _____ al estreno de la obra de mi amigo Juan. (ir)

2. Les sugiero a Uds. que _____ las entradas en la taquilla del teatro. (comprar)

3. El gerente (*manager*) del teatro exige que nosotros _____ y _____ cinco minutos antes de las siete y media de la noche. (entrar, sentarse)

4. Insisto en que todos nosotros _____ mucho y _____ ¡«Bravo»! después de cada acto. (aplaudir, gritar)

5. Yo espero que _____ muchas personas en el teatro. (haber)

6. También deseo que esta obra _____ mucho éxito. (tener)

7. Pedro y Luisa dicen que nosotros _____ a Juan al final de la obra. (abrazar)

8. ¡Ojalá que esta obra _____ por muchos meses en este teatro. (continuar)

9. Ojalá Juan _____ escribir más obras con mucho éxito. (poder)

¿El subjuntivo o el infinitivo? Traducción.

1. I suggest that you (*sing., fam.*) take your dog to the park.

_____

2. Alicia wants to eat with us tonight in the restaurant.

_____

3. Ana hopes that I'll buy the tickets to see a couple of new movies.

_____

4. Let's hope I can win this contest!

_____

5. My sister says that you're (*pl., form.*) not leaving the house now.

_____

6. The manager does not allow me to work on Saturdays.

_____

7. I forbid you (*sing., fam.*) to repeat these lies.

_____

8. The trainer insists that you (*sing., fam.*) run three miles.

_____

9. Does he prefer that I put all these documents on his desk?

_____

10. Why does the doctor recommend that you do not drink sodas?

_____

11. I wish I had a better job and made (**ganar**) more money now!

_____

12. I advise you (*sing., fam.*) to go to the bank today before five o'clock.

_____

13. We hope that you (*pl., form.*) are well and healthy.

_____

14. Louis and Joan want me to write a letter.

_____

15. I hope it does not rain tomorrow.

_____

EJERCICIO
19·3

Y en tu caso, ¿verdadero (V) o falso (F)?

1. _____ Deseo que llueva mañana.

2. _____ Quiero despertarme tarde todos los días de la semana.

3. _____ Necesito que mis amigos rieguen (*water*) el jardín.

4. _____ Prefiero que mis amigos olviden mi cumpleaños.

5. _____ Ojalá mi familia gane la lotería.

6. _____ Espero que nieve mucho mañana para quedarme en casa.

7. _____ Sugiero que mis vecinos no hagan mucho ruido por la noche.

8. _____ Insisto en que mis amigos me acompañen siempre cuando voy a una fiesta.

9. _____ Quiero que pierda mi equipo favorito de fútbol americano.

10. _____ Exijo que mis vecinos sean amables.

◆ Verbs that express doubt and uncertainty

dudar	*to doubt*
no creer	*to not believe*
no estar convencido, -a de	*not to be convinced about*
no estar seguro, -a de	*to not be sure about*
no pensar	*to not think*
no suponer(se)	*to not suppose*

Dudamos que tú **lleves** estas lámparas para tu sala.	*We doubt that you will take these lamps to your living room.*
Yo **no creo** que **compres** este auto fabuloso.	*I do not believe that you can buy this fabulous car.*
No estoy convencido de que Uds. **sean** miembros de nuestra familia.	*I am not convinced that you are members of our family.*
Lina **no está segura de** que le **devuelvan** su dinero.	*Lina is not convinced that they will return her money.*
El entrenador **no piensa que tú puedas** bajar de peso en dos semanas.	*The coach does not think that you can lower your weight in two weeks.*
No **se supone que** el huracán **afecte** a Puerto Rico.	*It is not thought that the hurricane will affect Puerto Rico.*

Most of the verbs on the previous list are expressed in the negative with **no**. In negative sentences the verb in the subordinate clause is in the subjunctive; otherwise the verb in the subordinate clause is in the indicative.

Ellos **no están seguros** de que Laura **trabaje** aquí.	*They are not sure that Laura works here.*
Ellos **están seguros** de que Laura **trabaja** aquí.	*They are sure that Laura works here.*
Yo **no creo** que Ud. **pueda** salir del hospital ahora.	*I do not think that you can leave the hospital now.*
Yo **creo que** Ud. **puede** salir del hospital ahora.	*I think that you can leave the hospital now.*

More about doubt, uncertainty, and conjunctions

Conjunctions are invariable: that is, they never change form. Their function is to connect words and phrases. They also connect the main clause to the subordinate clause. If the action in the subordinate clause that follows the conjunction is uncertain or doubtful, use the subjunctive in the subordinate. Some of the conjunctions in this list imply answers to questions such as *how?*, *when?* etc.

a menos que	*unless*	**hasta que**	*until*
antes (de) que	*before*	**mientras que**	*while*
aunque	*although, even if*	**para que**	*in order that, so that*
cuando	*when*	**sin que**	*without*
después (de) que	*after*	**tan pronto como**	*as soon as*
en caso de que	*in case*		

Salimos a las diez de la noche **a menos que tu hermano no llegue** aquí.	We will leave at ten o'clock tonight unless your brother does not get here.
No compraremos el apartamento **antes que el abogado lea** el contrato.	We will not buy the apartment before the lawyer reads the contract.
Tenemos que visitar a Anita **aunque llueva** mucho.	We need to visit Anita even if it rains a lot.
Cenaremos **después que Pedrito termine** la tarea.	We will have dinner after Pedrito finishes his homework.
Te ayudaré a limpiar la casa **para que tú descanses**.	I will help you clean the house so that you can rest.
Yo trabajaré con Ileana **hasta que ella salga** de la oficina.	I will work with Ileana until she leaves the office.
Carlos contestará **tan pronto como pueda**.	Carlos will answer as soon as he can.

In the following examples you see that the conjunctions **cuando** and **aunque** followed by the subordinate clause do not suggest uncertainty or doubt. Therefore, the indicative mood follows the conjunction.

| Juan siempre me contesta **cuando yo lo llamo**. | Juan always answers when I call him. |
| **Aunque** es barato, no vamos a comprar este sofá. | Even though it is not expensive, we are not going to buy this sofa. |

EJERCICIO
19·4

Dudas y posibilidades. *Complete each sentence with the appropriate form of the present subjunctive of the verb in parentheses.*

1. Dudo que tu equipo de fútbol _____ el partido hoy. (ganar)

2. No estamos convencidos de que Uds. _____ suficiente espacio en el maletero de su auto. (tener)

3. Marta y Rogelio no piensan que nosotros _____ llegar temprano a la cena. (poder)

4. Yo dudo que esto _____ un platillo volador. (ser)

5. Pedro no está seguro de que tu hermana _____ lista para salir conmigo. (estar)

6. Ellas no están convencidas de que estos zapatos _____ tanto dinero. (costar)

7. Tus padres no te dejan salir por las noches hasta que tú _____ buenas notas en la escuela. (recibir)

8. Luisa explica las palabras para que nosotros _____ palabras nuevas en español. (aprender)

9. Yo no voy al cine esta noche a menos que mis amigos _____ conmigo. (ir)

10. Regresaremos mañana después que Uds. _____ en el restaurante. (cenar)

11. Iré a tu casa este verano cuando mis padres _____una visita a mis abuelos. (hacer)

12. Luis estudia mucho en caso de que _____un examen esta semana. (haber)

Mentiras. Traducción. *Use the words in the* **Vocabulario útil** *for your translation.*

VOCABULARIO ÚTIL

able	**capaz**	*drawer*	**la gaveta, el cajón**
according to	**de acuerdo a**	*to be fired*	**estar despedido, -a**
to allow	**permitir**	*Good heavens!*	**caramba**
to beg	**pedir, rogar**	*insecure*	**inseguro, -a**
to be over	**terminar**	*on his/her knees*	**de rodillas**
colleague	**el/la colega**	*rule*	**la regla**
to commit a crime	**cometer un crimen**	*to stay, remain*	**quedarse**
conduct	**la conducta**	*truth*	**la verdad**

Good heavens! My friend Alicia cannot believe that this is happening again. Again, Julia is looking for something inside one of the drawers. I am sure that Julia needs my help. She never helps me unless she needs a favor. Julia thinks that she can use anything that her colleagues have in the office. My friends do not think that she is able to understand and follow the rules of conduct. They are on one of the walls near the entrance. Julia will not be fired until someone tells the truth. Now, Alicia is writing an anonymous note to her boss in order that he understand this problem. As soon as the boss reads the note, the truth will come out. I will believe it when I see the results. We doubt that the boss will allow Julia to work here. We do not believe that the boss will give her a letter of recommendation even if she begs on her knees. We will be happy when this is over.

_____

_____

_____

_____

_____

_____

_____

_____

_____

_____

_____

Verbs that express feelings and emotions

alegrarse de	*to be glad, happy*
sentir	*to be sorry, regret*
sorprenderse (de)	*to be surprised*
temer	*to fear, suspect*
tener miedo de	*to be afraid of, fear*

Ellos **se alegran de** que tú te **gradúes** este verano.	*They are happy that you will graduate this summer.*
Siento mucho que Uds. no **puedan** cenar conmigo.	*I am sorry that you cannot have dinner with me.*
¡Mi hija **se sorprende de** que sus amigas **estén** aquí!	*My daughter is surprised that her friends are here!*
Temo que no **pases** este examen de matemáticas.	*I am afraid that you may fail this math exam.*
Tengo miedo de que de los ladrones **roben** mi auto.	*I am afraid that the thieves may steal my car.*

More about emotions

To express emotions and feelings, you need a form of **estar** followed by an adjective. These are usually considered temporary conditions (you may want to review Chapter 3). Again, this calls for the subjunctive in the subordinate clause.

estar + adjective + **que** + a subordinate clause

Estamos encantados + **que participes** en esta reunión

We are delighted that you are participating in this meeting.

Estoy feliz que mi novio **venga** esta noche.	*I am happy that my boyfriend is coming tonight.*
Luisa **está preocupada que** tú **pierdas** el vuelo.	*Luisa is worried that you may miss the flight.*

Verbs that express a request

pedir (**e→ i**)	*to ask, request*
rogar (**o → ue**)	*to beg*
suplicar	*to implore*

Juan **pide** que Uds. **traigan** las sábanas a su cuarto.	Juan requests that you bring the bedsheets to his room.
Por favor, te **ruego** que **apagues** las luces.	Please, I beg you to turn off the lights.
¡Tenemos sueño, te **suplicamos** que no **enciendas** la televisión!	We are sleepy, we implore you not to turn on the television!

Las emociones y el subjuntivo. *Complete each sentence with the appropriate form of the present subjunctive of the verb in parentheses.*

1. Te pido que no _____ la hora de la cita mañana. (olvidar)

2. Marcia tiene miedo de que Uds. no _____ las cortinas en su cuarto. (colgar)

3. Yo le ruego a mi novio que no _____ la fecha de nuestra boda. (decir)

4. Juanita se sorprende de que nosotros _____ con ella ahora. (estar)

5. Te suplico que no _____ a ese chico horrible otra vez a la casa. (traer)

6. Los meteorólogos se sorprenden de que _____ venir estas tormentas. (poder)

7. Siento mucho que mis hermanos no _____ la Navidad conmigo el año que viene. (celebrar)

8. Estamos encantados de que Uds. _____ el piano en nuestra sala. (tocar)

9. Te ruego que tú me _____ para la cita con el dentista. (acompañar)

10. Estoy muy preocupado de que tú no _____ en este partido. (jugar)

11. Mis amigos temen que Raúl y Lidia no _____. (casarse)

12. Estamos muy felices de que nuestros hijos _____ sus cursos en la universidad. (terminar)

Esto es raro. Traducción. *Use the words in the **Vocabulario útil** for your translation.*

VOCABULARIO ÚTIL

again	**de vuelta**	*hairdresser's*	**el salón de la peluquería**
battery	**la batería**	*to give up*	**rendirse**
doorbell	**el timbre**	*noon*	**el mediodía**
to color (hair)	**teñirse (el pelo)**	*peephole*	**la mirilla**
either . . . or	**o... o**	*to ring the bell*	**tocar el timbre**
garage	**el taller mecánico**		

This is odd! It is seven o'clock in the morning and today is Saturday, a day to rest. Someone is ringing the doorbell of Pablo's home. Pablo opens the peephole and he is not surprised that his neighbor Rogelio comes so early. Pablo is afraid that Rogelio wants to get into his home. Marilú, Pablo's wife, asks him to open the door. Pablo gives up and opens the door. Rogelio is surprised that Pablo does not say good morning, but he is happy that Marilú is behind her husband. Rogelio suggests that either Marilú or Pablo take him to a mechanic. Rogelio needs a new battery for his car. Marilú doubts that she can help him unless Rogelio waits until noon. She has an appointment at the hairdresser's in order to color her hair. Now, Rogelio is looking at Pablo, and he begs him to help him as soon as possible. Fine: Pablo takes Rogelio to the garage but it isn't open. Rogelio gets out of the car. And with an ironic look Pablo leaves him there. He is not going to take him back. Let him take a cab! Good-bye!

_____

_____

_____

_____

_____

_____

_____

_____

_____

_____

_____

_____

_____

Impersonal expressions and opinions

Impersonal expressions that express possibility, doubt, uncertainty, necessity, emotion, or a command appear in the main clause. These types of impersonal expressions require the subjunctive in the subordinate clause. The pattern for impersonal expressions requires a form of **ser** + expression + **que** + a subordinate clause: **Es importante que escuches** las noticias (_It is important that you listen to the news_).

es dudoso que	_it is doubtful that_
es importante que	_it is important that_

es imposible que	*it is impossible that*
es (una) lástima que	*it is a shame / a pity that*
es mejor que / más vale que	*it is better that*
es necesario que	*it is necessary that*
es posible que	*it is possible that*
es probable que	*it is probable that*
es fantástico que	*it is fantastic that*
es increíble que	*it is incredible/unbelievable that*
es terrible que	*it is terrible that*

Es dudoso que **escribamos** esta carta esta noche.	*It is doubtful that we will write this letter tonight.*
Es importante que **guardes** una copia de este documento en tu oficina.	*It is important that you keep a copy of this document in your office.*
Es una lástima que no **tengas** acceso a la Internet en casa.	*It is a pity that you don't have access to the Internet at home.*
Es necesario que **aprendamos** otros idiomas.	*It is necessary that we learn other languages.*
Es muy **probable** que **llueva** mañana.	*It is very probable that it will rain tomorrow.*
Es mejor que **estudiemos** para pasar la prueba.	*It is better that we study for the test.*
¡Más vale que manejes (conduzcas) despacio en esta carretera!	*It is better that you drive slowly on this road!*

Some impersonal expressions express certainty in the main clause. In this case the verb in the subordinate clause is in the indicative.

es cierto que	*it is certain*
es verdad que	*it is true*
es obvio que	*it is obvious*

Es cierto que mis padres **vienen** hoy.	*It is certain that my parents come today.*
Es obvio que tú estás alegre.	*It is obvious that you are happy.*

EJERCICIO
19·8

Sugerencias para tener tu éxito en el trabajo. Traducción.

1. It is necessary that you think first and be patient (**tener paciencia**) before answering a question.

_____

2. It is important that you communicate your ideas frequently to your colleagues.

_____

3. It is much better that you attend all the meetings on time.

_____

4. It is fantastic that you take notes to help your group.

_____

5. It is terrible if you do not obey the regulations at work (**reglamento**) even if they are ridiculous.

_____

6. It is doubtful that you will get (**tener**) a raise unless you follow the rules.

_____

7. It is not likely that you can help all your colleagues.

_____

8. But it is better that you continue with your efforts.

_____

9. It is very likely that you will win the certificate of employee of the year.

_____

10. It is incredible that you do everything that is on this list!

_____

11. You are very persistent!

_____

12. And it is very obvious that you want to be successful.

_____

Uncertain antecedent

If the subject of the main clause (the antecedent) is vague or uncertain, use the subjunctive in the subordinate clause. If the antecedent is certain and known to exist, use the indicative in the subordinate clause.

Definite antecedent:	**Tengo amigos** que me **ayudan** mucho.	*I have friends who help me a lot.*
Uncertain antecedent:	**No tengo amigos** que me **ayuden** mucho.	*I do not have friends who help me a lot.*
Definite antecedent:	Carlos **encontró a alguien** que **habla** alemán y francés.	*Carlos found someone who speaks German and French.*
Uncertain antecedent:	Carlos **no encontró a nadie** que **hable** alemán y francés.	*Carlos did not find anyone who speaks German and French.*

Remember that the personal **a** needs to be placed before **alguien** (*someone*) and **nadie** (*nobody, no one*), even when their existence is uncertain.

Ellos no conocen **a nadie** que **viva** en Caracas.	*They do not know anyone who lives in Caracas.*
¿Conoce Ud. **a alguien** que **pueda** comprar mi auto?	*Do you know anyone who can buy my car?*

EJERCICIO
19·9

Traducción.

1. I want to buy a home that is far from the city.

   _____

2. We need a car that does not cost too much.

   _____

3. My nephews want a puppy that is mischievous (**travieso**).

   _____

4. We have neighbors who make a lot of noise.

   _____

5. Where can I find a piano that looks like yours?

   _____

6. My friends have a maid who makes excellent enchiladas.

   _____

7. Is there anyone here who can help me now?

   _____

8. No, there is no one here who can open the door to the building.

   _____

The imperfect subjunctive

As we saw in Chapter 19, the subjunctive mood is used with ideas that show uncertainty, doubt, demand, desire, emotions, among other feelings. The imperfect subjunctive is used in exactly the same sense, but it refers to the past, not the present.

Let's consider the two sentences below and the tenses that appear in the main and subordinate clauses.

Nosotros **dudamos** que Marta **compre** el piano.	*We doubt that Marta is buying the piano.*
Nosotros **dudábamos** que Marta **comprara** el piano.	*We doubted that Marta would buy the piano.*

The first sentence shows the indicative present tense **dudamos** in the main clause and the present subjunctive **compre** in the subordinate clause. In the second sentence, the indicative imperfect tense **dudábamos** is in the main clause. It refers to the past, so therefore **comprara** in the subsidiary clause is in the imperfect subjunctive. But first we need to review the formation of the imperfect subjunctive and the circumstances in which we need to use it.

Formation of the imperfect subjunctive

The first step is to remember the third person plural of the indicative preterit tense and then drop the -**ron** ending. This will give you the stem for forming the imperfect subjunctive.

comprar	compraron	**compra-**
vender	vendieron	**vendie-**
abrir	abrieron	**abrie-**

The second step is to add the appropriate endings. There are actually two possible sets of endings for the imperfect subjunctive, which apply to all three conjugations.

-**ra** endings: -**ra, ras, ra, -ramos, -rais, -ran**
-**se** endings: -**se, -ses, -se, -semos, -seis, -sen**

Either set of endings may be used and both mean the same, but the **-ra** endings are used more frequently in the Spanish-speaking world, and we will be using them from now on, as the following examples from each conjugation of regular verbs show.

-ar verbs: comprar	compraron	comprara, compraras, comprara, compráramos, comprarais, compraran
-er verbs: vender	vendieron	vendiera, vendieras, vendiera, vendiéramos, vendierais, vendieran
-ir verbs: abrir	abrieron	abriera, abrieras, abriera, abriéramos, abrierais, abrieran

Note that a written accent is required in the **nosotros** form of both sets of endings. The stress falls on the vowel before the subjunctive ending.

Querían que nosotros **comiéramos** con ellos.	*They wanted us to eat with them.*
Deseaban que nosotros **llegásemos** pronto.	*They wished that we would arrive soon.*
Ella dudaba que nosotros **estuviéramos** aquí.	*She doubted that we would be here.*

As with the present subjunctive that we reviewed in Chapter 19, verbs that have a change in spelling in the preterit tense maintain that spelling change in the stem of the imperfect subjunctive:

destruir	destruyeron	**destruye-**
dirigir	dirigieron	**dirigie-**
distinguir	distinguieron	**distingui-**
estar	estuvieron	**estuvie-**
ir	fueron	**fue-**
hacer	hicieron	**hicie-**
querer	quisieron	**quisie-**
recoger	recogieron	**recogie-**
tener	tuvieron	**tuvie-**
ver	vieron	**vie-**

Uses of the imperfect subjunctive

In order to use the imperfect subjunctive in the subordinate clause, the main clause must be in a past tense.

- Main clause in the preterit

¿No **cenaste** antes de que tus vecinos **llegaran**?	*Did you not eat before your neighbors arrived?*
Tú **sugeriste** que **jugáramos** en el parque.	*You suggested that we play in the park.*
Fue horrible que no **estuvieras** tomando esa medicina.	*It was terrible that you were not taking that medicine.*

- Main clause in the imperfect

> **Era necesario** que **practicáramos** antes de jugar.
>
> *It was necessary that we practice before we played.*

> Alicia **necesitaba** que le **dieran** una copia de su documento.
>
> *Alicia needed them to give her a copy of her document.*

> Ellos **querían** que yo **descansara**.
>
> *They wanted me to rest.*

- Main clause in the past perfect

> El maestro no **había autorizado** que los estudiantes **salieran** del aula.
>
> *The teacher did not allow the students to leave the classroom.*

EJERCICIO
20·1

¡Práctica! *Complete each sentence with the appropriate form of the imperfect subjunctive (-**ra** ending) of the verb in parentheses.*

1. Queríamos que tú _____ con nosotros. (venir)

2. Nos pidieron que nosotros _____ a sus padres. (acompañar)

3. Mi jefe nunca permitía que los empleados _____ más de una hora para la hora del almuerzo. (tomar)

4. Yo había salido con mis amigos para que ellos _____ disfrutar su visita a mi ciudad. (poder)

5. Sentimos mucho que María no _____ a tocar el violín. (aprender)

6. Nosotros nunca queríamos que _____ tanta gente en la playa. (haber)

7. Laurita y Pablito dudaban que la fiesta de mi aniversario de bodas _____ divertida. (ser)

8. Me dijeron que yo _____ quedarme con ellos en su casa durante mi visita. (deber)

9. Y también me rogaron que yo _____ a mi hermana Rosa. (traer)

10. Fue una pena que Rosa no _____ con nosotros. (estar)

11. Queríamos que Uds. _____ de una manera apropiada y agradable. (comportarse)

12. Fue fabuloso que ellos _____ a todos sus amigos el día de su (abrazar) llegada.

Traducción. *Use the appropriate form of the imperfect subjunctive (-ra ending) or an infinitive, as needed.*

1. I wanted you (*sing., fam.*) to bring two bottles of soda.

   _____

2. You (*sing., fam.*) wanted us to cook rice and beans.

   _____

3. It was ridiculous that we had so much food for five people.

   _____

4. Alberto and Carlos were not sure that their friends would come.

   _____

5. It was a pity that we spent so much.

   _____

6. They wanted to divide the amount of the expenses by three.

   _____

7. I was not sure that they would pay me.

   _____

8. Carlos begged me to wait until the weekend.

   _____

9. Did he prefer not to pay? Of course!

   _____

10. No one believed that Carlos would return the money to me.

   _____

Y en tu caso, ¿verdadero (V) o falso (F)?

1. _____ Deseaba que mis padres me regalaran un auto nuevo.

2. _____ Quería que mis amigos me ayudaran con las tareas.

3. _____ Prefería que mi novio/novia no supiera mi edad.

4. _____ Necesitaba que mis vecinos dejaran un espacio para aparcar mi auto.

5. _____ Ojalá mi familia ganara mucho dinero en la lotería.

6. _____ Quería que hubiera mucha paz y no más guerras.

7. _____ Quería que mis vecinos no sacaran mi ropa de la lavadora en el sótano.

8. _____ Siempre insistía en que mis colegas llegaran temprano al trabajo todos los días.

9. _____ Yo quería que mi familia se mudara a México.

10. _____ Yo siempre autoricé a mis colegas a que usaran mi computadora en la oficina.

The conditional in the main clause: Contrary-to-fact conditions

As seen in Chapter 16, one of the uses of the conditional is to express a contrary-to-fact action—that is, a hypothetical statement or events that are not probable. In some textbooks they are called hypothetical *if*-clauses. Usually all *if*-clauses with a past tense are considered hypothetical and therefore require the subjunctive, as demonstrated in the following sentences.

Si yo **tuviera** más dinero, no **ahorraría** tanto. *If I had more money I would not save so much.*

Si tú **estudiaras** más, **tendrías** más oportunidades en el futuro. *If you studied more, you would have more opportunities in the future.*

These *if*-clauses indicate actions or events that may be possible, yet most probably will not happen.

EJERCICIO
20·4

¡Práctica otra vez! *Complete each sentence with the appropriate form of the imperfect subjunctive (-ra ending) of the verb in parentheses.*

1. Serías trilingüe si tú _____ italiano. (estudiar)

2. Nadie te creería si tú no _____ la verdad. (decir)

3. Llamaría a mi madre si yo _____ enfermo. (estar)

4. Podríamos disfrutar más si nosotros _____ un televisor grande. (tener)

5. No esperaría a mis amigos si ellos _____ muy tarde al aeropuerto. (llegar)

6. ¿Qué harías si yo _____ el piano en tu casa? (tocar)

7. María se casaría si su novio le _____ la mano. (pedir)

8. Le pediría ayuda a mis padres si yo no _____ pagar el alquiler. (poder)

9. Nosotros iríamos de compras si no _____ mucha gente. (haber)

10. Estaríamos felices si Uds. nos _____ al cine. (llevar)

Traducción. *Use the* **-ra** *endings of the imperfect subjunctive.*

1. If I had a friend here now I would be happy.

_____

2. I would not sing a song if you do not play the guitar.

_____

3. I would introduce you to my sister if you were not so shy.

_____

4. I would not answer the question if I did not know the answer.

_____

5. If it weren't raining, we would have dinner on the terrace.

_____

6. This house would be worth (**valer**) one million dollars if it had a pool in the backyard.

_____

7. It would be a miracle if my friends helped me to finish my homework.

_____

8. If you were stronger you would be able to play better.

_____

9. If the suitcase were bigger, I would not take it with me.

_____

10. If I were a liar, who would believe me?

_____

Y en tu caso, ¿verdadero (V) o falso (F)?

1. _____ Si tuviera que trabajar los domingos, yo renunciaría (*resign*).

2. _____ No ayudaría a mis colegas si se rieran de mí.

3. _____ Sería terrible si no aprendiera español.

4. _____ Si alguien pusiera su auto en mi espacio de parqueo, llamaría a la policía.

5. _____ Sería increíble si yo pudiera tocar el violín.

6. _____ Si mis amigos me pidieran un favor, yo lo haría.

7. _____ Si yo pudiera, viviría en Madrid.

8. _____ Si yo tuviera más tiempo, me entrenaría para un maratón en Nueva York.

9. _____ Yo no pudiera correr rápido si no practicara tres veces a la semana.

10. _____ Sería fantástico si yo comprara una computadora nueva.

EJERCICIO
20·7

Sueños son sueños. Traducción. *Use the words in the* **Vocabulario útil** *for your translation.*

VOCABULARIO ÚTIL

broken, broken-down	**descompuesto, -a**
dishes (pl.)	**la vajilla**
happy	**placentero, -a**
in-laws	**los suegros**
fairy tale	**el cuento de hadas**
to achieve, meet	**lograr**
to call, warn	**avisar**
to be lucky	**tener suerte**
to wash (dishes, clothes)	**fregar**
unknown	**desconocido, -a**

Everyone would like his/her life to be pleasant. For example, if it had not rained today I would be very happy. If I worked fewer hours in my office, I would have more time to relax and to watch movies on my TV. If my parents lived close to me, they would help me every week to clean the house. If I found one thousand dollars, I would invite my friends to have dinner in a fabulous restaurant. If I had the luck not to have to go back to my job, I would travel to an unknown place. I would not have to open my door if my in-laws were visiting without warning us by telephone. If I were rich I would not have this horrible, old and broken-down car. I would be the queen of the house if I did not have to wash the dishes. It would be a perfect world! It would a fairy tale if I could keep everything under my control. But dreams are dreams, nothing else.

_____

_____

_____

_____

_____

Answer key

1 Subject pronouns and the present tense

1·1 1. Ella 2. ellas 3. Él 4. Ellos 5. Nosotros / Nosotras 6. Ustedes 7. ellos
8. Ustedes

1·2 1. canto 2. escucha 3. bailan 4. descansan 5. preparamos 6. lavas
7. compartes 8. confío 9. deciden 10. responden 11. entra 12. recibe
13. suman 14. dividimos 15. rompen 16. echo 17. sufre 18. toca
19. terminamos 20. descansan

1·3 1. Necesitas descansar. 2. Él habla, yo escucho. 3. Estudia chino y español también.
4. Nosotros gastamos mucho dinero. 5. Ustedes compran camisas caras.
6. Trabajo cinco días a la semana. 7. Ellas bailan todos los sábados. 8. Mi hermana
toca el piano, pero yo toco la guitarra.

1·4 1. Abrimos la tienda a las ocho. 2. Ustedes conversan con los clientes.
3. Respondemos sus preguntas. 4. Repartes los folletos de publicidad. 5. Describes las
cualidades de nuestros productos. 6. Trabajamos mucho aquí. 7. Ustedes pasan
mucho tiempo con su familia. 8. Pero admito que trabajo muchas horas.

1·5 Vivo en Tampa, en la Florida. Cerca de nuestra oficina hay un restaurante cubano muy
popular, «Casa Manolo». Mis amigos y yo comemos en este restaurante. Caminamos al
restaurante y leemos el menú con los platos especiales del día. El camarero siempre
describe los platos especiales. Abre una botella de agua mineral para la mesa. Mauricio y
yo siempre comemos frijoles negros, un plato típico cubano. Un buen almuerzo termina
con un delicioso café negro y dulce, un café cubano. Después del almuerzo regresamos a la
oficina.

1·6 1. Protejo 2. Convenzo 3. Exijo 4. Recojo 5. Escojo 6. Ejerzo
7. Dirijo 8. Distingo

1·7 Answers will vary.

1·8 Mi esposa Delia trabaja en una tienda lujosa en el centro. Yo ayudo en casa. Recojo la
basura todas las mañanas. Mi hija Mariana siempre coopera conmigo. Hoy convenzo a
Mariana: ella cose los botones de mi camisa, por fin. Mariana y yo sembramos vegetales en
el patio y trabajamos duro. Siempre escojo productos orgánicos para las comidas. Mi hijo,
Sam, nunca finge estar feliz. Él casi nunca gana cuando juega al béisbol con su equipo. Pero
siempre exige sus derechos. Sam y yo tomamos un refresco y hablamos de los deportes
después del partido. Esa es mi familia.

2 Present tense irregular verbs

2·1 1. desciende 2. despierta 3. enciende 4. Empieza 5. hierve 6. Friega
7. atraviesa 8. Comienza 9. sienta 10. cierra

2·2 1. comenzar; comienza 2. divertir; divierte 3. sentir; sienten 4. defender; defienden
5. recomendar; recomiendan 6. empezar; empieza 7. advertir; advierte
8. cerrar; cierran

2·3 1. Bernardo y José suelen ayudar a sus amigos. 2. Cuando llueve, José me recoge en mi oficina. 3. Bernardo recuerda mi cumpleaños todos los años. 4. Almuerzo con José frecuentemente. 5. Juegan al golf los domingos. 6. Cuando juego con ellos, yo cuento los puntos para el resultado. 7. José vuela a Costa Rica todos los veranos / cada verano. 8. Usualmente vuelve a Albuquerque después de una semana.

2·4 1. h 2. i 3. c 4. d 5. f 6. e 7. b 8. g 9. j 10. a

2·5 1. consigue 2. pide 3. sonríen 4. siguen 5. sirve 6. compite 7. impide 8. huye 9. despide 10. concluye

2·6 Answers will vary.

2·7 1. digo 2. tiene 3. pongo 4. sé 5. viene 6. doy 7. es 8. estoy 9. traigo 10. oímos 11. hace 12. propongo

2·8 Answers will vary.

2·9 1. Conozco 2. Sé 3. conozco 4. Conozco 5. sé 6. Sé 7. Conozco 8. conozco

2·10 Mi prima Julia viene a mi casa los viernes por la noche. Yo salgo de mi tienda temprano y conduzco mi carro al supermercado. Escojo vegetales verdes, lechuga, tomates y otros productos. Yo pertenezco a una organización, «Salud es vida». Voy a las reuniones dos veces al mes. Cuando llego a casa, pongo las bolsas en la cocina y empiezo a cocinar rápido. Suena el timbre de la puerta y abro la puerta. Veo a Julia y le doy un beso. Siempre le ofrezco a Julia la oportunidad de cocinar la cena. Si mi vecino Felipe oye nuestras voces o huele la comida, viene a mi casa. Él tiene una guitarra. Trae la guitarra y toca dos o tres canciones. A eso de la medianoche digo hasta luego. ¡Tengo sueño! Hasta pronto.

3 Ser and estar, and adjectives

3·1 1. a 2. b 3. e 4. d 5. c 6. g 7. d 8. f

3·2 1. c 2. d 3. h 4. f 5. e 6. b 7. g 8. a

3·3 1. a 2. b 3. d 4. a 5. a 6. c 7. c 8. c 9. e 10. d

3·4 Answers will vary.

3·5 1. es 2. está 3. están 4. estamos 5. es, está 6. está 7. es 8. es, estoy

3·6 1. Llego a las cuatro de la mañana. 2. Son las tres y diez de la tarde. 3. La clase termina a las nueve de la mañana. 4. Empiezo a trabajar a las doce de la tarde / al mediodía. 5. Salgo a las nueve menos cuarto de la mañana. 6. Preparo la cena a las seis y cuarto de la tarde.

3·7 1. interesante, fantástico 2. grandes, feroces 3. exóticas, frescas 4. templado, frío 5. especial, raras 6. medicinales, tóxicas

3·8 joven, alta, negros, grandes, madrileña, elegante, clásica, alegre, norteamericano, andaluz, antigua, agradable, blancas, amarillas, rojas, dormilón, haragán, largas, cansado, popular, varios

3·9 1. Madrileña. 2. Joven, alta, (ojos) negros (y) grandes, elegante. 3. Pianista. 4. Alegre, dormilón, haragán. 5. Antigua, agradable.

3·10 1. Soy una buena persona. 2. Vivo en Miami y soy mexicano. 3. Soy agradable y cortés. 4. Mi apartamento está en el primer piso. 5. Tengo algunos problemas con mi vecina. 6. Ella es quisquillosa y chismosa. 7. Ella es una influencia mala en mi edificio. 8. Siempre está de mal humor

3·11 1. son 2. es 3. está 4. están 5. estoy 6. estoy 7. son 8. es 9. está 10. está

3·12 1. trae; Ana está trayendo una camisa a la cajera. 2. mira; La cajera está mirando la etiqueta y el precio. 3. ayuda; Juan está ayudando a una clienta. 4. llora, pide; Un niño está llorando y está pidiendo agua. 5. duerme; La hermanita está durmiendo en un coche. 6. lee; Un chico está leyendo un mensaje de texto en su teléfono. 7. busca; Un cliente está buscando una corbata roja. 8. sale; El gerente está saliendo de su oficina. 9. cierra; La secretaria está cerrando la puerta. 10. entran; Dos jóvenes están entrando al elevador. 11. salen; Dos chicos están saliendo de la tienda. 12. voy; Yo estoy yendo a la casa de Marcos ahora.

4   The near future, nouns, and articles

4·1   1. Mañana por la mañana vamos a visitar un museo en Madrid.   2. Más tarde voy a caminar por la ciudad.   3. Mañana por la tarde Laurita va a ver a sus amigos de Barcelona.   4. La semana que viene Laurita y yo vamos a viajar a Sevilla.   5. La semana siguiente tú y Laura vais/van a regresar a California.   6. Mis padres van a mudarse de Los Ángeles a Miami el año que viene.

4·2   Answers will vary.

4·3   1. N   2. Y   3. N   4. N   5. Y   6. Y   7. N   8. N   9. Y   10. N   11. Y   12. N   13. Y   14. Y   15. Y   16. Y   17. N   18. Y   19. N   20. N

4·4   1. El idioma español es muy popular ahora en los Estados Unidos.   2. Los papeles en mi escritorio son viejos.   3. ¡El viaje es fantástico!   4. Las sillas en la terraza son cómodas.   5. La crisis financiera afecta a muchas personas.   6. ¿Cuál es el tema de este artículo del periódico?   7. ¡Los chocolates son una tentación!   8. Mi temor es real: ¡odio las cucarachas y los mosquitos!   9. A veces la tristeza es un problema.   10. Algunas costumbres son muy raras.

4·5   1. el   2. la   3. el   4. la   5. el   6. la   7. el   8. el   9. el   10. el   11. el   12. el   13. el   14. la   15. el

4·6   1. ¡Qué locura! Ahora es difícil decir la verdad.   2. ¡Una mentira es una cosa horrible!   3. La ambición, en español, significa el deseo de ser rico/a.   4. La generosidad ayuda a una comunidad.   5. La ignorancia no resuelve un problema.   6. ¡Vamos a vencer la pobreza y la tristeza!

4·7   1. unos franceses   2. unos arroces   3. unos boletines   4. unas veces   5. unas órdenes   6. unos sillones   7. unas estaciones   8. unos olores   9. unas águilas

4·8   1. una computadora   2. unos sillones   3. un televisor   4. unas costumbres   5. un dilema   6. unas notas   7. un camino   8. unas canciones

4·9   Answers will vary.

5   Adverbs and comparisons

5·1   1. deprimentemente   2. tranquilamente   3. preocupadamente   4. ansiosamente   5. tristemente   6. seguramente   7. hábilmente   8. felizmente   9. sensiblemente   10. orgullosamente   11. emocionadamente   12. tímidamente   13. agradablemente   14. sentimentalmente   15. amablemente

5·2   1. tímidamente   2. positivamente   3. moderadamente   4. sarcásticamente   5. dolorosamente   6. sinceramente

5·3   mucho, barato, claro, alto, bastante, rápido, justo, algo, igual, mal, diariamente, Seguramente, regularmente

5·4   1. mucho, barato   2. claro, no (hablan) alto.   3. algo, mal.   4. Claramente, altamente, rápidamente, justamente, igualmente, malamente, fácilmente.

5·5   1. e   2. d   3. b   4. f   5. c   6. g   7. a

5·6   1. Por primera vez voy a un concierto de guitarra clásica con mi amigo Pedro.   2. Voy de mala gana. No entiendo la música clásica.   3. De repente, escucho al / a la guitarrista en el teatro con pasión.   4. Sé la letra de memoria y la canto en voz baja.   5. Por fin sé que la música clásica no es siempre aburrida.

5·7   1. cortés, cortésmente   2. elegante, elegantemente   3. alegre, alegremente   4. veloz, velozmente   5. intenso, intensamente   6. nuevo, nuevamente   7. veraz, verazmente   8. general, generalmente   9. desgraciado, desgraciadamente   10. indudable, indudablemente

5·8   1. La geografía no es menos interesante que la historia.   2. La ciudad San Diego es tan agradable como la ciudad Santa Ana.   3. Las frutas tropicales no son más baratas que las frutas de California.   4. El río Grande es menos caudaloso que el Mississippi.   5. Las ciudades del sur de los EE.UU. son más antiguas que las ciudades del norte.   6. Las carreteras son menos anchas que las autopistas de peaje.   7. Las personas del sur de los Estados Unidos son tan amables como las personas del oeste del país.   8. Las montañas Rocosas son más impresionantes que las montañas del sureste.

5·9   Answers will vary.

5·10 Voy al dentista dos veces al año. El doctor / La doctora Salazar es agradable. La higienista me limpia los dientes cuidadosa y suavemente. Toma los rayos x cada dos años. Ahora tengo dos caries en una muela y necesito dos empastes. No tengo dolor de muela pero necesito una corona también. Por suerte / Afortunadamente tengo una póliza de seguro dental. El doctor / La doctora Salazar dice que no necesito anestesia para la corona. Mi peor problema es que me desmayo cuando oigo el zumbido del taladro. ¡Necesito a mi mejor amigo aquí! ¡Desafortunadamente / Desgraciadamente / Por desgracia, soy un/a cobarde!

6 Gustar and verbs like gustar

6·1 1. le gustan 2. Le fascinan 3. nos interesa 4. os encantan 5. Les agrada 6. Te disgusta 7. nos molestan 8. les apasionan

6·2 1. duelen 2. preocupa 3. quedan 4. sobra 5. toca 6. hacen falta 7. importa 8. bastan

6·3 le encantan; le fascina; le importa; le aburre; le molestan; le bastan; le quedan; le duele; le hace falta

6·4 1. Le gustan los deportes y las actividades al aire libre. 2. A Pablo le fascina esquiar y patinar sobre hielo. 3. No, a Miguel no le importa si hace frío o calor. 4. A Julia le aburre quedarse en casa. 5. Hoy le duele la cabeza.

6·5 1. durante 2. hasta 3. alrededor de 4. con 5. para 6. delante de 7. desde 8. Según

6·6 Answers will vary.

6·7 1. ¡Nunca necesitas mi ayuda! 2. ¿No ha venido ninguna persona a tu casa? 3. No conozco a nadie como tú. 4. Tampoco conozco ninguna de tus costumbres. 5. No conocemos a ninguno de tus primos. 6. Tus amigos ni te visitan ni te saludan. 7. No necesitas nada, creo yo. 8. Tampoco sabes que yo soy muy cortés. 9. No, no te puedo ayudar ahora.

6·8 A veces pienso que el tiempo libre me gusta / agrada. Pero cuando leo la sección «Ocio» en el periódico, no sé qué hacer. Tenemos muchas opciones. A nadie le gusta hacer cola para comprar las entradas para una película nueva. Yo las compro en línea mientras juego un videojuego en mi computadora. Nunca juego los juegos de mesa ni el billar. Veo «La ruleta de la suerte». Algunos concursantes apuestan y ganan mucho dinero. ¡Me encanta /me fascina mirar / ver los programas de televisión!

7 Reflexive verbs and reflexive pronouns

7·1 1. se levanta 2. se ducha 3. se cepillan 4. nos maquillamos 5. se desvisten / os desvestís 6. se secan

7·2 1. Me acuesto temprano todas las noches. 2. Antes de acostarme me desvisto. 3. Después me pongo el pijama / piyama. 4. Me duermo a eso de las diez de la noche. 5. A las seis de la mañana me despierto. 6. Pero me levanto media hora más tarde. 7. Después me ducho con agua fría. 8. Me seco el pelo. 9. No me afeito. 10. Me cepillo los dientes por la mañana en casa. 11. Me maquillo un poco. 12. Me miro en el espejo. 13. Me visto antes de las ocho de lunes a viernes. 14. Al final / Por fin me lavo las manos y estoy listo/a.

7·3 Answers will vary.

7·4 1. se aburre 2. se parecen 3. va 4. duermen 5. parece 6. pone 7. duerme 8. se pone 9. va 10. lleva

7·5 1. Tus comentarios me aburren. 2. Me aburro cuando estoy solo/a. 3. Voy a ir dormir ahora. 4. Molestas a mi perro. 5. El dinero no cae del cielo. 6. Mi amigo Alex despierta a sus hijos. 7. Voy a llevar a mi mamá al dentista. 8. Usualmente / Por lo general yo no me despierto tarde los fines de semana. 9. Me enojo si no duermo bien. 10. Me quito los zapatos y me pongo las zapatillas / pantuflas. 11. Me llevo muy bien con mi jefe/a. 12. ¿Cuándo te vas? 13. Creo que vas a visitar a Mila. 14. Pongo mis toallas en el baño. 15. Llevo a mis perros al parque todos los días.

7·6 1. se burla, se ríe 2. se da cuenta 3. nos negamos 4. se queja 5. se atreven 6. nos olvidamos 7. me sorprendo

7·7 1. ¿Te acuerdas de mi amigo Carlos? 2. ¡Me burlo del novio de mi hermana! 3. No me arrepiento de mis comentarios. 4. Ahora nos enteramos de tus mentiras. 5. No me quejo de tus preguntas. 6. ¡Me sorprendo porque estás aquí! 7. Me doy cuenta de que mi auto / mi carro no está en el garaje. 8. ¡Me muero de sed! 9. No me atrevo a jugar golf con tu padre. 10. ¡Me olvido de todo! 11. Nos negamos a mudarnos a otra ciudad.

7·8   De acuerdo a mi nutricionista, nosotros necesitamos escribir dos listas.

Una lista de los buenos hábitos: acostarse temprano y dormir ocho horas, levantarse temprano y dar gracias por un nuevo día, atreverse a cambiar la rutina diaria, olvidarse del pasado y pensar en el futuro, enterarse de las necesidades de nuestros amigos, negarse a ser haragán / vago y acordarse de que la vida es corta.

Y una lista corta de malos hábitos: quejarse de todo, no darse / no darnos cuenta de nuestra buena fortuna, burlarse de los hábitos de otras personas y olvidarse que mañana es otro día.

8   Direct and indirect object pronouns and commands

8·1   1. los; Rosa los recita.   2. las; Manolita está componiéndolas / Manolita las está componiendo.   3. le; Mari no le lleva los cuadernos.   4. los; Almodóvar los hace reír.   5. la; Yo la llevo para Marcela.   6. la; Martín no quiere conocerla. Martín no la quiere conocer.   7. los; Gustavo los toca.   8. nos; ¿Vas a incluirnos en la lista? / ¿Nos vas a incluir en la lista?

8·2   1. les; Ángel está comprándoles creyones. Ángel les está comprando creyones.   2. les; Ali está llevándoles regalos. Ali les está llevando regalos.   3. les; Raquel va a distribuirles la comida. Raquel les va a distribuir la comida.   4. les; Lalo y María no van a cantarles canciones mexicanas. Lalo y María no les van a cantar canciones mexicanas.   5. le; Lola nunca puede prestarle atención. Lola nunca le puede prestar atención.   6. le; Margarita no quiere recitarle sus poemas en el ayuntamiento. Margarita no le quiere recitar sus poemas en el ayuntamiento.

8·3   1. las, les; Carmen se las compra.   2. los, les; Ella se los prepara.   3. la, le; Pedrito se la da.   4. las, nos; Raúl nos las plancha.   5. les, los; Carmen y Raúl están dándoselos. Carmen y Raúl se los están dando. 6. los, les; Marta se los compra.   7. las, les; ¿Marcos se las envió?   8. las, me; Manuel me las trae. 9. las, le; Yo se las compro.   10. las, les; Martín está enviándoselas. Martín se las está enviando.

8·4   1. cambia; no cambies   2. pide; no pidas   3. viaja; no viajes   4. vuelve; no vuelvas   5. duerme; no duermas   6. piensa; no pienses   7. corre; no corras   8. sufre; no sufras   9. lee; no leas   10. vende; no vendas

8·5   1. Usa la computadora nueva.   2. No borres mis notas.   3. Pon el papel en la impresora.   4. Por favor, no contestes el teléfono.   5. ¡Ve a tu oficina ahora!   6. Guarda estos papeles, por favor.   7. No uses estas llaves viejas.

8·6   1. Pon la maleta / la bolsa en el piso / el suelo.   2. Sal a las ocho y media hoy.   3. Ten cuidado porque está lloviendo.   4. Ven temprano a la clase.   5. Sé amable / cortés.   6. Ve al mercado y compra pan. 7. Di la verdad ahora.   8. Haz tu trabajo con cuidado / cuidadosamente.

8·7   1. No pongas tu maleta en mi asiento.   2. No dejes los papeles en el suelo / el piso.   3. No tengas problemas con tus amigos.   4. No vengas tarde al teatro.   5. ¡No seas ridículo/a!   6. No vayas ahora a la playa.   7. ¡No digas mentiras!   8. No hagas comentarios inapropiados.

8·8   1. lea / no lea   2. conteste / no conteste   3. use / no use   4. reciba / no reciba   5. asista / no asista 6. vaya / no vaya   7. sea / no sea   8. descanse / no descanse

8·9   1. Doblen a la derecha.   2. Sigan las instrucciones.   3. Busquen la salida 45 en la autopista de peaje. 4. Manejen dos millas después de la salida.   5. Lleguen a la calle Olmedo, número 114.   6. Aparquen al frente de nuestro edificio de apartamentos.   7. Toquen el timbre a la entrada del edificio.

8·10   1. leed, no leáis   2. dormid, no durmáis   3. sufrid, no sufráis   4. pensad, no penséis   5. viajad, no viajéis   6. vivid, no viváis   7. leed, no leáis   8. caminad, no caminéis   9. conseguid, no consigáis 10. haced, no hagáis

8·11   1. lo, les; Léeselo.   2. la, le; Anita, escríbesela.   3. lo, le; Dáselo.   4. los, me; No me los compren.   5. los, le; Díganselos.   6. los, le; Sra. Blanco, cuénteselos.   7. la, les; Ábransela.   8. la, les; No se la envíen.

9   Demonstrative and possessive adjectives and pronouns

9·1   1. Este   2. esos   3. aquellos   4. esos   5. Aquellos   6. este   7. aquellos   8. aquellas 9. Estas   10. Estos

9·2   1. Esta joyería está vacía.   2. ¡Ah, estos anillos de diamantes deben costar una fortuna! 3. Esos aretes no son baratos.   4. Usen / usad aquel elevador/ascensor para ir al segundo piso. 5. En ese escaparate tienen perlas y esmeraldas.   6. A aquellos caballeros les encantan los relojes de Suiza. 7. Estoy listo/a para comprar ese brazalete de oro.

9·3 1. mi carro / mi auto 2. tu bicicleta 3. sus patines 4. su taxi 5. nuestra motocicleta 6. sus cercas 7. sus / vuestros vecinos / sus, vuestras vecinas 8. su / vuestro jardín 9. mis árboles 10. nuestro edificio

9·4 1. el mapa mío 2. el calendario tuyo 3. el boleto suyo 4. la mochila suya 5. los asientos nuestros 6. las maletas suyas 7. El auto nuestro 8. los sombreros vuestros

9·5 1. estos 2. aquellas 3. esos 4. estas 5. aquel 6. aquella 7. esa 8. estos 9. aquel 10. estas

9·6 1. ¿Por qué quieres esto? 2. Esta es mi sombrilla y esa es la sombrilla de Manuel. 3. Tengo un impermeable pero me gusta este. 4. Molly no tiene un sombrero. Ella necesita aquel. 5. Y aquello, ¿qué es?

9·7 1. las nuestras. 2. la tuya 3. las nuestras 4. el suyo 5. el suyo 6. los vuestros 7. las suyas 8. la nuestra

10 Idiomatic verbal phrases

10·1 1. d 2. a 3. f 4. b 5. c 6. g 7. e 8. h

10·2 1. Estoy a punto de terminar estas respuestas en esta hoja. 2. Estoy por salir. 3. No estoy de acuerdo con tus ideas. 4. No estoy de buen humor si no tomo la siesta por la tarde. 5. Estaré de vuelta a eso de la medianoche. 6. No estoy apurado/a. Puedo esperar unos minutos.

10·3 1. hacer un viaje 2. hacer un recado 3. hacer una visita 4. hacer caso 5. hacerse daño 6. hacer una lista 7. hacer fresco 8. hacer la maleta

10·4 Answers will vary.

10·5 1. g 2. a 3. h 4. b 5. i 6. e 7. f. 8. c 9. d 10. j

10·6 1. ¿Tienes frío o calor? 2. Tienes miedo a la aguja. 3. No tienes confianza en el cirujano / la cirujana. 4. No tienes miedo a la oscuridad. 5. El/La siquiatra tiene razón. Tú estás cuerdo /a. 6. Tienes prisa para salir de la clínica. 7. ¿Tienes sueño? Yo apago la luz. 8. Tienes suerte. Esta enfermera / Este enfermero es excelente. 9. Tienes cuarenta años y tienes buena salud. 10. Ahora tienes hambre y estás listo /a para ir a casa.

11 Interrogatives and exclamations

11·1 1. ¿Qué estás haciendo ahora? 2. ¿A quién / quiénes ves aquí? 3. ¿Quiénes son tus amigos? 4. ¿Cuál de estas mesas quieres? 5. ¿Cuáles de estos juegos prefieres, el ajedrez o el dominó? 6. ¿Cuánto dinero pagas por estos zapatos ridículos? 7. ¿Cuánta paciencia tienes con tus amigos? 8. ¿Cuántos libros lees cada año? 9. ¿Cuántas amigas tienes en tu vecindario? 10. ¿Cómo puedes leer y escuchar a la misma vez? 11. ¿Cuándo vas a California? 12. ¿Dónde está mi dinero? 13. ¿Adónde voy esta noche? No sé. 14. ¿Por qué no tengo un trabajo? Soy perezoso/a. 15. ¿Por qué uso este libro todos los días? ¡Me ayuda a aprender español!

11·2 1. ¿Quién es Ud.? 2. ¿Dónde vive Ud.? 3. ¿Cuántos hijos tiene Ud.? 4. ¿Cómo se llaman ellas? / ¿Cuáles son sus nombres? 5. ¿Cuántos años tienen? 6. ¿Por qué viaja Ud. a Miami? 7. ¿Cuándo regresa Ud. a Venezuela? 8. ¿Cuál es su profesión?

11·3 1. Adónde 2. Dónde 3. Cuándo 4. Qué 5. Cuántos 6. Cuántas 7. Cuáles 8. Cuál 9. Cómo 10. Cuánta

11·4 1. Cuál 2. Qué 3. qué 4. Cuáles 5. qué 6. Cuáles 7. cuál 8. Qué 9. Qué

11·5 1. qué 2. cuánto 3. Cuántos 4. Qué 5. cuántos 6. Qué 7. Qué 8. Qué

11·6 1. ¿Qué? Max quiere invertir dos mil dólares en la bolsa de valores. 2. ¿Por qué no? Max no quiere ahorrar el dinero en el banco. 3. Él cree que puede ganar dinero en seis meses. ¡Buena suerte! 4. ¡Qué locura! La economía no está estable ahora. 5. ¿Qué tengo yo en mi cartera de inversiones? 6. ¿Cuántas acciones de compañías excelentes de los EE.UU.? 7. ¡Qué alegría / felicidad! Hoy la bolsa de valores gana. 8. Pero, ¿qué va a pasar mañana? ¡Quién sabe! 9. ¿Cómo podemos seguir la situación de la economía en todo el mundo? 10. ¿Quién es tu asesor/ asesora?

12 Regular verbs in the preterit tense

12·1   1. salió   2. abrí   3. preparamos   4. llamaron   5. saludó   6. comimos   7. compartimos
       8. nos sentamos

12·2   Answers will vary.

12·3   1. Ayer perdí un anillo de oro y lo busqué en mi apartamento.   2. Me equivoqué.   3. ¿Dónde coloqué mi
anillo?   4. Empecé a buscar mi anillo en la sala.   5. Recé por/durante unos minutos.   6. Entonces apagué
la luz y salí de la sala.   7. Saqué un traje y un par de pantalones de mi auto /carro.   8. Más tarde los colgué
en un armario/closet.   9. Entonces tropecé con una maleta grande.   10. Toqué algo en el suelo/piso y
encontré mi anillo.   11. Empecé a sentirme mucho mejor.   12. Entonces desempaqué mi maleta.

12·4   Answers will vary.

12·5   1. contribuyeron   2. oímos   3. destruyó   4. oyó   5. se cayó   6. proveyó   7. huyó   8. incluyeron
       9. distribuyó   10. leyeron

12·6   1. empezó, llovió   2. lanzó, alcancé   3. pagué, compartí   4. sacó, grabó   5. coloqué, encontré
       6. buscó, descubrió   7. me alegré, comprendí   8. aceptó, tomó   9. terminó, salimos   10. leyó, decidió
       11. escribió, trajo   12. saludó, colocó   13. empecé, llamó   14. invitó, entregué

13 Irregular and stem-changing verbs in the preterit tense

13·1   1. condujeron   2. hizo   3. cupieron   4. tuvieron   5. vinieron   6. estuvieron   7. trajo   8. puse
       9. anduvimos   10. pudieron

13·2   Querido Pepe,

La semana pasada te dije que me gusta leer libros de historia. Ayer hice una lista de lo que sé acerca de la
historia de México. Después, fui a la biblioteca y pude encontrar un par de libros interesantes en español. Los
traje a casa y los puse en mi escritorio. Empecé a revisar los títulos de los capítulos. Unos minutos después,
Jaime vino a visitarme y nos sentamos para leer. Encontramos algunas palabras difíciles.
Desafortunadamente, mi gata Lili nos distrajo varias veces. Esta mañana tuve que tomar una decisión.
Te voy a hacer varias preguntas acerca de palabras en español y los temas de historia.

Hasta pronto,

Rocío

13·3   1. Mis amigos y yo fuimos a un partido de béisbol anoche.   2. Vimos el partido en una pantalla grande en
el estadio.   3. Yo fui uno de los miembros del equipo de béisbol en mi escuela secundaria.   4. Dimos las
gracias a Julio. Él se puso en la cola por dos horas para comprar las entradas.   5. ¿Viste a tus jugadores
favoritos?   6. ¿Pudiste sentarte al lado de tus amigos?   7. Vi a una joven bella / preciosa. ¡Agarró una
pelota sin guante!   8. ¿Quién fue el gran ganador ayer? ¡Fui yo! Mi jugador favorito ganó el partido.

13·4   Answers will vary.

13·5   1. se vistió   2. midió   3. se despidió   4. siguió   5. consiguió   6. eligió   7. pidió

13·6   La semana pasada encontré una carta en el baúl de mi abuela. Dentro del sobre vi diez monedas viejas de oro.
Puedo entender mensajes en español, inglés y francés pero no en alemán. Hace unas semanas conocí a Hans,
un vecino, y es de Alemania. Quise hacerle algunas preguntas a Hans. Hans no puede ayudarme porque supe
ayer que está de vacaciones. Quiero saber los detalles de esta carta misteriosa. No quiero hablar acerca de esta
carta con amigos ni con miembros de mi familia. No quiero regalarle las monedas de oro a nadie.

13·7   1. quise   2. trajo   3. redujo   4. Hubo   5. estuvieron   6. pudo   7. tradujo   8. vimos

14 The imperfect tense

14·1   1. ibais / iban   2. se despertaba   3. iba   4. vivían   5. éramos   6. veían   7. llevaba   8. se ponía
       9. sentía   10. podía, padecía   11. conocíamos   12. querían   13. era   14. sabía, querían

14·2   1. Cuando tenía dieciséis años, vivía en un pueblo pequeño.   2. Mi hermano y yo corríamos a un lago
cerca de nuestra casa.   3. Durante el verano muchos de nuestros amigos nadaban en el lago.   4. El lago
era bello / bonito pero el agua siempre estaba fría.   5. Yo siempre quería dormir debajo de un árbol.
       6. Me sentía cómodo/a y seguro/a allí.   7. Mi hermano y yo siempre queríamos disfrutar un verano largo
y delicioso.

14·3   1. b   2. a   3. c   4. e   5. e   6. d   7. c   8. a   9. b   10. e

14·4   1. tenía   2. dibujaba   3. iba   4. hacía   5. tenía   6. había.   7. entraba   8. escuchaba   9. veía   10. leía   11. quería   12. pensaba   13. era

14·5   1. Mis padres y yo generalmente visitábamos varias ciudades en los Estados Unidos cuando era una jovencita.   2. Cada año viajábamos a lugares como Fresno, St. Augustine y otras ciudades.   3. Muchas veces mi padre alquilaba un auto / carro grande.   4. En aquellos días me encantaba quedarme por unos días en ciudades diferentes.   5. A veces conocía a nuevos amigos como Fernando.   6. Todas las semanas yo quería hablar con Fernando.   7. ¡Era tan cómico! Varias veces yo escribí su nombre y dibujé un corazón en un papel.   8. Fernando me enviaba muchas cartas.   9. Yo siempre me sentía feliz leyendo sus cartas.   10. Fernando y no nos casamos y ahora recordamos aquellos días cuando éramos jóvenes.

14·6   1. Él me interrumpió mientras yo hablaba.   2. Eran las cuatro en punto cuando Rosa y yo nos encontramos en la floristería.   3. El auto se rompió mientras yo manejaba a la estación de trenes.   4. Tú todavía esperabas a tus amigos cuando ellos llegaron una hora más tarde.   5. El Dr. Ruiz estaba conmigo cuando otro paciente gritó en el pasillo.   6. Luis leía una revista cuando su hermano lo llamó.   7. Mis amigos escuchaban una canción cuando sonó el timbre de la puerta.   8. ¿Quién vino a hablar a Alex cuando él estaba en su oficina?

14·7   Esta mañana me desperté tarde. Bostecé muchas veces, estaba feliz, me sentía optimista. Entonces abrí la ventana de mi habitación y estiré los brazos. Los semáforos no funcionaban. Por suerte no había mucho tráfico en la calle y veía pocos peatones. Salí a recoger mi periódico. No lo abrí. No leí las noticias horribles. Fui a la cocina y preparé mi desayuno. Quería dormir y roncar. De repente sonó el despertador y me desperté. ¡Ay, Dios mío! No era sábado, domingo. No era día feriado. ¡Qué mala suerte! Era un sueño.

15   The future tense

15·1   Answers will vary.

15·2   1. empezará   2. será   3. bajará   4. destruirá   5. mostrará   6. oirán   7. caerá   8. deberán   9. protegerán   10. mejorará

15·3   Answers will vary.

15·4   1. estará   2. tendremos   3. costarán   4. harán   5. vendrán   6. hará   7. pondrá   8. querrán   9. tendrán   10. Habrá   11. Valdrá

15·5   1. deberás   2. Tendrás   3. Conocerás   4. ganarás   5. encontrarás   6. Recibirás   7. Podrás   8. ahorrarás   9. perderás

15·6   1. Te opondrás   2. obtendrán   3. dispondré   4. supondrán   5. mantendremos   6. repondrá   7. detendrá   8. obtendrá

15·7   1. estará   2. será   3. se llamará   4. podrá   5. tendrá   6. pertenecerá   7. costará   8. Lloverá   9. se sentirán   10. querrán   11. dejará

15·8   Mila cumplirá cinco años pronto. Esta noche su abuela Alina leerá el cuento de hadas favorito de Mila: Cenicienta. Mila se dormirá y soñará con Cenicienta. Mila sabe este cuento de memoria. Cenicienta ayudará a sus hermanastras miserables y seguirá las órdenes de su madrastra. Después sus hermanastras irán a la sala de baile en el palacio. Afortunadamente, Cenicienta tendrá la ayuda de su hada madrina: con una varita mágica hará un vestido bello, un par de zapatillas de cristal y un carruaje de lujo para ir al palacio. Cenicienta conocerá al príncipe y bailará con él. A las doce menos cuarto, regresará a casa. Cenicienta dejará caer una de las zapatillas de cristal. Y después el príncipe la encontrará y se casarán.

16   The conditional tense

16·1   Answers will vary.

16·2   1. viajaría   2. preferiríamos   3. subirían   4. jugarían   5. estudiaríamos   6. oirían   7. iría   8. bebería   9. comerías   10. pediría

16·3   1. ¿Gastarías todo el dinero?   2. ¿O ahorrarías el diez por ciento por lo menos?   3. ¿Qué comprarías para tu casa?   4. ¿Ayudarías a tu familia?   5. ¿Buscarías otro tipo de trabajo?   6. ¿Donarías un poco de tu dinero para ayudar a tu comunidad?   7. ¿Disfrutarías unos meses en casa?   8. ¿Viajarías a otros países?   9. ¿Te gustaría esquiar en Colorado?   10. ¿Invitarías a tus amigos para viajar contigo?

16·4   1. Sería posible encontrar a nuestros amigos en San Juan.   2. Pondría tu maleta grande en el maletero. 3. Tu maleta no cabría en un asiento del auto/carro.   4. ¿Podríamos llegar al aeropuerto temprano mañana?   5. Yo diría a eso de las cinco de la tarde.   6. Saldríamos a las tres y media pero vivimos cerca del aeropuerto.   7. No perderíamos el vuelo a San Juan.   8. Valdría la pena disfrutar un largo fin de semana en Puerto Rico.

16·5   1. vendrían   2. se quedarían   3. pondría   4. cocinaría   5. invitaríamos   6. sería   7. tendrían 8. querrían   9. diría   10. valdría

16·6   1. componer; compondrías   2. obtener; obtendrían   3. poder; podría   4. disponer; dispondría 5. contener; contendría   6. poder; podrían   7. proponer; propondrías   8. mantener; mantendrías

16·7   1. b.   2. c   3. a   4. g   5. f   6. d   7. j   8. e   9. h   10. k   11. i   12. l

17   The present perfect and past perfect tenses

17·1   1. No he hablado con mis amigos hoy.   2. Mis primos / Mis primas nunca han estado conmigo por dos semanas.   3. Rita se ha duchado pero no se ha lavado el pelo / el cabello.   4. ¿Me has enviado un mensaje para ir a un partido de fútbol?   5. Carla jamás/nunca me ha contestado/respondido una pregunta acerca de su edad.   6. ¿Les ha comentado a ustedes / a vosotros(as) que ella es más joven que yo?   7. Nunca he entendido/comprendido por qué ella es tan reservada.   8. No nos hemos conocido antes. Ha sido un placer.

17·2   Answers will vary.

17·3   1. ha roto   2. he descubierto   3. ha dicho   4. se han opuesto   5. ha encubierto   6. ha devuelto   7. ha hecho   8. he escrito   9. he descrito   10. he puesto   11. he vuelto   12. he deshecho   13. he resuelto

17·4   1. disolver; han disuelto   2. distraerse; se han distraído   3. morir; ha muerto   4. freír; ha frito 5. imprimir; ha impreso   6. descomponerse; se ha descompuesto   7. poder; he podido   8. ver; hemos visto   9. disolver; has disuelto   10. proponer; has propuesto

17·5   1. V   2. F   3. V.   4. F   5. F   6. V   7. F   8. V   9. F   10. V

17·6   1. habían proveído   2. había devuelto   3. se habían distraído   4. había visto   5. había roto 6. se había descompuesto   7. habían hecho   8. habíamos descubierto

17·7   1. yo había comprado   2. había tenido   3. habían ayudado   4. habían interesado   5. había visto 6. se habían negado   7. había llevado   8. había entregado   9. había recibido   10. había deseado

17·8   Yo le había pedido un favor a un amigo mío, Mario. Necesitaba una carta de recomendación para ingresar en un club muy exclusivo y carísimo. No le había dicho muchos detalles a Mario. Pero le había dicho que mis antepasados eran aristócratas y tenían mucho dinero. Cuando conocí a Boni siempre había querido visitar lugares fabulosos y había pensado presentarla a mis amigos en un lugar impresionante, en ese club exclusivo. Yo había tenido la impresión de que Boni era algo extrovertida. Después de salir varias veces con Boni, me había dado cuenta de que Boni es sincera. Por eso, decidí enfrentar la verdad: no tengo que impresionar a nadie.

18   The passive voice

18·1   1. abiertas   2. traídos   3. dibujados   4. vendidos   5. distribuidos   6. preparado   7. celebrada 8. invitados   9. aprobada   10. donados

18·2   1. Las invitaciones habían sido enviadas.   2. Las invitaciones fueron hechas por algunos de los miembros de la familia.   3. Las direcciones de los sobres fueron escritas por la hermana de la novia.   4. Un contrato ha sido firmado por la banda de música.   5. El menú fue creado por un chef peruano.   6. El salón de baile fue decorado con muchas flores.   7. El día de la boda fue elegido por la novia.   8. Los regalos fueron enviados por los amigos del novio y la novia.   9. El champán fue servido para un brindis.   10. Muchas fotos fueron tomadas en el salón de baile.

18·3   1. Se han cerrado   2. se han escrito   3. se han leído   4. Se han prohibido   5. Se han vendido   6. se ha resuelto   7. se han aceptado   8. Se han enviado   9. Se han puesto   10. Se ha roto

18·4   Answers will vary.

18·5 1. ¿Cómo se dice «gracias» en francés? 2. ¿Dónde se venden juguetes? 3. ¿Cuándo se aumentarán los precios? 4. ¿Dónde se compran libros escritos en japonés? 5. ¿Qué se habla aquí en esta tienda? 6. ¿Cuándo se sirve el desayuno en el hotel? 7. ¿Dónde se aceptan cupones de descuento? 8. ¿Cómo se dice «lo siento» en portugués?

18·6 1. ¿Cómo se puede vivir sin amor? 2. ¡Podemos vivir sin amor pero no sin dinero! 3. ¿Por qué se habla tanto de / acerca de una crisis económica? 4. Se dice que es mejor pensar de una manera positiva y no pesimista. 5. ¿Dónde se puede encontrar amigos/as? 6. Se dice que es más fácil encontrar amigos/as nuevos/as en una página de la Web.

18·7 —¿Cómo se entrena un nadador / una nadadora para competir en natación en las Olimpiadas?

—Por lo general, se entrena con un entrenador / una entrenadora profesional.

—¿Cuántos días a la semana?

—Se sabe que todos los atletas se entrenan seis días a la semana y descansan un día.

—Pero, ¿cuántas horas se nada en la piscina?

—Muchas horas y se debe comprometer a descansar y dormir.

—¿Qué se espera de un/una atleta que quiere nadar en las próximas Olimpiadas?

—Se espera mucho: tener confianza en sí mismo/misma, ser perseverante y mantenerse en buena forma, físicamente y mentalmente.

—¿Se debe tener un horario todos los días?

—Sí, se necesita para acostumbrarse a una rutina diaria.

—Por favor, deme un ejemplo de un horario diario.

—Por supuesto. Se levanta temprano, después los ejercicios de calentamiento. Se usa un cronómetro para medir el tiempo y la rapidez cuando nada.

—Muchas gracias y hasta pronto.

19 The present subjunctive

19·1 1. vayan 2. compren 3. entremos, nos sentemos 4. aplaudamos, gritemos 5. haya 6. tenga 7. abracemos 8. continúe 9. pueda

19·2 1. Yo sugiero que tú lleves a tu perro al parque. 2. Alicia quiere cenar con nosotros esta noche en el restaurante. 3. Ana espera que yo compre las entradas para ver un par de películas nuevas. 4. ¡Ojalá yo pueda ganar este concurso! 5. Mi hermana dice que no salgan Uds. de la casa ahora. 6. El gerente no me permite trabajar los sábados. 7. Te prohíbo que repitas estas mentiras. 8. El entrenador insiste en que tú corras tres millas. 9. ¿Él prefiere que yo ponga todos los documentos en su escritorio? 10. ¿Por qué el doctor / la doctora te recomienda que no tomes refrescos? 11. ¡Yo deseo tener un trabajo mejor y ganar más dinero ahora! 12. Te aconsejo que vayas al banco hoy antes de las cinco en punto. 13. Ojalá / Espero que todos Uds. estén bien y saludables. 14. Louis y Joan quieren que yo escriba una carta. 15. Ojalá / Espero que no llueva mañana.

19·3 Answers will vary.

19·4 1. gane 2. tengan 3. podamos 4. sea 5. esté 6. cuesten 7. recibas 8. aprendamos 9. vayan 10. cenen 11. hagan 12. haya

19·5 ¡Caramba! Mi amiga Alicia no puede creer que esto pase otra vez. Otra vez, Julia está buscando algo dentro de una de las gavetas. Estoy seguro/-a de que Julia necesita mi ayuda. Ella nunca me ayuda a menos que ella necesite un favor. Julia piensa que ella puede usar cualquier cosa que tienen sus colegas en la oficina. Mis amigos no creen que ella sea capaz de entender y seguir las reglas de conducta. Están en una de las paredes cerca de la entrada. Julia no será despedida hasta que alguien diga la verdad. Ahora, Alicia está escribiendo una nota anónima a su jefe para que él entienda este problema. Tan pronto como el jefe lea la nota, la verdad saldrá. Yo lo creeré cuando yo vea los resultados. Dudamos que el jefe le permita a Julia trabajar aquí. No creemos que el jefe le escriba una carta de recomendación aunque ella ruegue de rodillas. Estaremos felices cuando esto termine.

19·6 1. olvides 2. cuelguen 3. diga 4. estemos 5. traigas 6. puedan 7. celebren 8. toquen 9. acompañes 10. juegues 11. se casen 12. terminen

19·7 ¡Esto es raro! Son las siete de la mañana y hoy es sábado, un día para descansar. Alguien toca el timbre de la casa de Pablo. Pablo abre la mirilla y no se sorprende de que su vecino Rogelio venga tan temprano. Pablo tiene miedo de que Rogelio quiera entrar a su casa. Marilú, la esposa de Pablo, le pide que abra la puerta. Pablo se rinde y abre la puerta. Rogelio se sorprende de que Pablo no diga «buenos días» pero se alegra de que Marilú esté detrás de su esposo. Rogelio sugiere que Marilú o Pablo lo lleve a un mecánico. Rogelio necesita una batería nueva para su carro / auto. Marilú duda que ella pueda ayudarlo a menos que Rogelio espere hasta el mediodía. Ella tiene una cita en la peluquería para que le tiñan el pelo. Ahora, Rogelio mira a Pablo y ruega que lo ayude tan pronto como sea posible. Bien; Pablo lleva a Rogelio al taller mecánico pero no está abierto. Rogelio sale del auto. Y con una mirada irónica Pablo lo deja allí. No lo va a llevar a casa. ¡Que tome un taxi! ¡Adiós!

19·8 1. Es necesario que pienses primero y que tengas paciencia antes de contestar una pregunta. 2. Es importante que comuniques tus ideas a menudo con tus colegas. 3. Es muchísimo mejor que asistas a todas las reuniones a tiempo. 4. Es fantástico que tomes notas para ayudar a tu grupo. 5. Es terrible que no obedezcas los reglamentos en el trabajo aunque sean ridículos. 6. Es dudoso que tengas un aumento a menos que sigas las reglas. 7. No es probable que puedas ayudar a todos tus colegas. 8. Pero más vale / Es mejor que continúes con tus esfuerzos. 9. Es muy posible que ganes el certificado del empleado del año. 10. ¡Es increíble que hagas todo lo que aparece en esta lista! 11. ¡Eres muy persistente! 12. Y es muy obvio que tú quieres tener éxito.

19·9 1. Quiero comprar una casa que esté lejos de la ciudad. 2. Necesitamos un auto que no cueste demasiado. 3. Mis sobrinos quieren un perro que sea travieso. 4. Tenemos vecinos que hacen mucho ruido. 5. ¿Dónde puedo encontrar un piano que se parezca al tuyo? 6. Mis amigos tienen una criada que hace enchiladas excelentes. 7. ¿Hay alguien / una persona aquí que me pueda ayudar ahora? 8. No, no hay nadie aquí que pueda abrir la puerta del edificio.

20 The imperfect subjunctive

20·1 1. vinieras 2. acompañáramos 3. tomaran 4. pudieran 5. aprendiera 6. hubiera 7. fuera 8. debiera 9. trajera 10. estuviera 11. se comportaran 12. abrazaran

20·2 1. Yo quería que tú trajeras dos botellas de refrescos. 2. Querías que cocináramos arroz y frijoles. 3. Era ridículo que tuviéramos tanta comida para cinco personas. 4. Alberto y Carlos no estaban seguros de que sus amigos vinieran. 5. Fue una pena que gastáramos tanto. 6. Querían dividir la cantidad de los gastos entre tres. 7. No estaba seguro/a que ellos me pagaran. 8. Carlos me suplicó que yo esperara hasta el fin de semana. 9. ¿Él prefería no pagar? ¡Por supuesto! 10. Nadie creía que Carlos me devolviera el dinero a mí.

20·3 Answers will vary.

20·4 1. estudiaras 2. dijeras 3. estuviera 4. tuviéramos 5. llegaran 6. tocara 7. pidiera 8. pudiera 9. hubiera 10. llevaran

20·5 1. Si tuviera un amigo aquí ahora estaría feliz. 2. Yo no cantaría una canción si tú no tocaras la guitarra. 3. Te presentaría a mi hermana si tú no fueras tan tímido. 4. No contestaría la pregunta si no supiera la respuesta. 5. Si no lloviera, cenaríamos en la terraza. 6. Esta casa valdría un millón de dólares si tuviera una piscina en el patio. 7. Sería un milagro si mis amigos me ayudaran a terminar mi tarea. 8. Si tú fueras más fuerte, podrías jugar mejor. 9. Si la maleta fuera más grande no la llevaría conmigo. 10. Si fuera mentiroso/a, ¿quien me creería?

20·6 Answers will vary.

20·7 Todo el mundo querría / quisiera que su vida fuera placentera. Por ejemplo, si no lloviera hoy, yo estaría muy feliz. Si trabajara menos horas en la oficina tendría mucho más tiempo para descansar y ver películas en mi tele. Si mis padres vivieran cerca de mí, me ayudarían todas las semanas a limpiar la casa. Si encontrara mil dólares invitaría a mis amigos a cenar en un restaurante fabuloso. Si tuviera la suerte de no tener que regresar a mi trabajo, viajaría a un lugar desconocido. No tendría que abrir la puerta de la casa si mis suegros nos visitaran sin avisarnos por teléfono. Si fuera rica no tendría este auto horrible, viejo y descompuesto. Yo sería la reina de la casa si no tuviera que fregar la vajilla. ¡Sería un mundo perfecto! Sería un cuento de hadas si pudiera tener todo bajo mi control. Pero los sueños son sueños, nada más.